Ken —

Working for B

been a defining moment in my

life.

I'm a better person, more

focused on how I can contribute

to others & make a difference.

Thank you for all you have done

& continue to do to inspire

others to be their best.

all the best —

DEFINING MOMENTS

of

Courage

6611 N 64th Place, Paradise Valley, AZ 85253
www.TechPressPublishing.com

First TechPress Publishing hardcover edition April 2012

Designed by Craig & Charlotte Jorgensen
Editor: Patti McKenna

Manufactured in the United States of America

ISBN 978-0-9854484-0-0

To your current or potential **defining moment** living within you that holds the power to inspire another individual to take a step forward with

COURAGE.

Your *story* is waiting to be written.

A portion of the proceeds from the sale of this book will be dedicated to youth empowerment programs by donation to the ***Economic Empowerment Foundation***

Endorsements

"Defining Moments of Courage proves that with slight edge steps you can create any life you want—but not all at once. You must understand that it is the little steps, compounded over time, that do make a difference. And you must learn that the things you do every single day—the things that don't look dramatic or don't look like they matter—do matter. Ultimately, one courageous step forward can make ALL the difference."

JEFF OLSON *Author of The Slight Edge*

"Defining Moments of Courage walks you through many of the most important lessons in life. You can either try to figure out these life lessons on your own or you can dive into this book, awaken your courage and start living your ultimate life today. Just remember, its your choice to create your ultimate life and Defining Moments of Courage gives you the proven steps to take on your journey."

JIM BUNCH *Founder of The Ultimate Game of Life*

"The Defining Moments shared in this book each share an insight as how an individual can inspire another to move forward to achieve a result and trust in the process of becoming a leader in their respective community. Having an understanding of how key insights, feelings and values motivate behavior has impacted how our TRIBE at WD-40 Company has evolved on our own path to success. At WD-40 Company we are encouraged daily to embrace learning moments that take us one step forward in the sandbox to see what Defining Moments we can create."

GARRY RIDGE *President and CEO, WD-40 Company*

CONTENTS

Foreword

DICTIONARIES DEFINE A "defining moment" as an occurrence that typifies or determines all related events that follow. In real life, defining moments can come in all shapes and sizes, persons, places or things. This book is a wonderful collection of inspirational stories that will help you have the courage to create or respond to the defining moments in your life. Learning from the mistakes and successes of others can help give you direction and tools to make your journey that much easier.

I remember when I first had the idea to start the *Chicken Soup for the Soul*® book series I didn't know how I was going to bring about the vision I held in my heart. All I knew was that these stories were so important to offer the world. Since that first book was published in 1993, I have seen the magic of what the right story at the right time can do to transform a life, heal a broken heart and inspire courageous action.

I am excited that a whole new generation of successful people have come together to share their stories of their defining moments so that you, too, can be inspired to surrender to your destiny and have the courage to create the life of your dreams.

The fact that you picked up this book entitled *Defining Moments of Courage* means it is probably safe for me to assume that you have made a determined start to create your life by design rather than live it by default. You can feel at ease, knowing that within these pages, you will gain an in depth understanding of how to stay focused on your goals, how to create an environment that will support your dreams, how to share your authentic voice even when there is a chance for ridicule, and how to own your personal power so that you can lead a successful and fulfilling life.

As you read through these stories of defining moments and study the lessons contained within them, I ask you to think about how the goals, attitudes, convictions, actions, and experiences that each author shares relate to you and contemplate how they can be applied to your life, your work, and your dreams. Take what resonates with you and apply it to your current situation. The only thing that will change your life in the future are the decisions you make and the actions you take today. So apply what you learn in these pages. Remember, in the end the road traveled depends on many things, but most importantly it depends on you. DM

JACK CANFIELD

Co-creator of *Chicken Soup of The Soul*® series
New York Times Bestselling Author

"The *time* comes in every life when there's a **fork** in the road.

Which path will you CHOOSE?"

Introduction

TURNING POINTS : *Why Not?*

A TURNING POINT in your life can be created by a traumatic event like an automobile accident or sudden health problem like a heart attack or diagnosis of malignant cancer. But it can also be created just as easily by a simple decision you make, albeit seemingly unimportant at the time, but with hindsight it ultimately reveals itself as a very significant decision…creating a "turning point" in your life.

As you read the stories in this book, you will find some that pull at your heart, others that hit you between the eyes, and still others that seem unreal in comparison to your own life. But we all make decisions every day, and you never know when the decision you make today may redirect the rest of your life.

In 1979, I was 25 living in Atlanta and miserable…even though I was a rising star in the Big Eight Accounting Firm where I worked. It seemed that I was either in the car driving to work or working. I had no time for a social life and kept thinking that if I was going to be working that hard, it should be for something I owned. I had grown up in an entrepreneurial home and seen my parents build businesses and invest in real estate. But my plan had been different. My parents dream was that I would get a college degree and climb the professional corporate ladder somewhere...and things were going well for me according to that plan...except I was miserable.

My own entrepreneurial spirit hit me over the head one night. A client called me on the phone and offered me an ownership position in a company he was investing in located in New Hampshire. It had an innovative new technology, and I had the opportunity to get in on the ground floor. How exciting! So I remember sitting on my bed with a tablet, writing the pros and cons of changing professions.

Did it have a large upside? Yes

Could I always come back to public accounting? Yes

This was as far as I got, when suddenly my hand took over and wrote across the top of the page "WHY NOT?"

I stared at the page for the longest time...and realized I couldn't answer that question. Instead of being a conservative accountant wanting all the answers to the question "WHY?," I decided to take a leap of faith and say, "Why Not!" I made the decision **at that moment** to accept my client's (soon to be partner's) offer...and I was off to New Hampshire...a place I had never been. But that was only the beginning of the story.

It was quite exciting moving to a new state with the new title of Chief Financial

Officer of a company. I found an apartment right on the ocean (yes, New Hampshire has coastline) and jumped in with both feet. I made a lot of friends and was having a great time. My goal was to straighten out the company's financials and position it to come out of bankruptcy so it could accept my client's funding for a new technology that was going to set the computer and recording industries on fire!

So you may be asking, how did it work out? Not exactly according to any plan I had written or imagined. Within just a couple of months, I had uncovered an absolute mess…financials that were filled with errors and omissions, a computer system in shambles, and risky decisions that I felt bordered on corruption. When voiced, my concerns fell on deaf ears. I was terrified and feared if I stayed I might be risking my professional credentials as a CPA. What a colossal mistake I had made. I felt like a stupid fool and was too embarrassed to call my old accounting firm. I took a couple of weeks off to contemplate what my next career move would be. My self-esteem had disappeared…going from being on the top of the world just months earlier to hiding from it.

I knew I had to leave the company but was still overwhelmed with shame for making such a stupid move. It seemed I could answer the question, "Why Not?" quite easily at that point. I knew I had to leave…I just didn't know where to go or what to do.

The day I returned to the company, I found lawyers at our offices, lawyers from the opposing side of a legal action that had been started well before I had joined the company. They were performing "discovery," which means they were looking through our documents to find evidence to support their claims in the case.

I had not been involved in the legal aspects of the case but knew it had to do with some ongoing patent litigation. (For you lawyers out there, it was a very unusual case, and the judge had ordered extraordinary discovery procedures—which just exacerbated my concerns about the company.) The lawyers had been kind enough to wait for me to return to go through my office and apparently had "elected" one attorney to search my office. His name was Michael Lechter.

Yes, I met my future husband when he was "going through my drawers!"…literally! He was sitting in my desk chair when I came in, and we shook hands over my desk… and there was an electric shock that we both felt. It truly was "Love at first sight!"

So even though I had already decided to leave a company that I had discovered might put my professional credentials at risk, I now knew I had to leave it quickly because I had just fallen instantly in love with someone on the opposite side of my company in litigation. The plot thickened.

Thankfully, the love-at-first-sight reaction was a mutual experience, and Michael asked me to move to Maryland, where he lived. So now I knew where I was going…but still didn't know what I would be doing. Michael and I were married nine months later and are celebrating 32 years together this year.

You might think that the moment I met Michael was the "turning point" in my life…

but to me, it was more like an answer to a question, "What and where is the next chapter in my life?" The actual turning point was when I was sitting on my bed in Atlanta that night and asked myself, "Why not?"

At that moment, I had decided to conquer the fear of the unknown… instead of asking "Why?," I chose to ask myself, "Why Not?" It has become the guiding principle in my life ever since.

The actual decision to go with the company was a colossal mistake from a business point of view, but it was the absolute right decision for the rest of my life. As Napoleon Hill said, "Every adversity, every failure, every heartache carries with it the seed on an equal or greater benefit."

I have made plenty of mistakes in my life and had several turning points that defined the person I have become. My oldest son went off to college in 1992 and got himself into credit card debt within the first few months. I was so angry at him, but even more so at myself. I thought I had taught him about money…I had taught him the lessons my parents had taught me. But when I went to college, I didn't have credit cards, and while my son had been with me when I used my credit cards, he was not with me when I paid them off each month. My husband and I refused to bail him out, and it took him seven years to get out of debt and repair his credit rating. I am proud to say that today he is as passionate as I am about teaching financial literacy to young people and business owners. Along the way, he also found his own passion and incredible talent as a teacher and coach and now coaches others to find and build their

own success stories.

My son's credit card debacle turned out to be another turning point in my life. My anger over the lack of financial education in schools became my passion, and I dedicated the rest of my professional career to creating financial education tools and teaching the importance of taking control of one's financial life. This may not have happened had my son not gotten into so much debt. Again, I asked myself, "Why Not?" Why not do something about what made me so mad? So instead of being embarrassed about my son's experience, I used it as a catalyst to define the direction of my career.

And they say…the rest is history. A few years, later I co-authored *Rich Dad Poor Dad* and 14 other books in the Rich Dad series and built the Rich Dad Company to become an international voice in financial empowerment…believing that it was my life's work and most important accomplishment. But it turned out to be a mere stepping stone as there was much more for me to do.

In 2007, there was yet another turning point in my life. At the height of our success at the Rich Dad company, I found myself miserable once again. My personal mission was no longer aligned with my partners' in the Rich Dad organization, and I made the decision to leave this very successful company. I am sure you have heard the expression, "When one door closes, another opens." My life has certainly been a living example of that phrase.

Little did I know that within just a few months of leaving the Rich Dad Organization, several things would happen that would reveal that my career in financial education had truly just started.

First, I formed my own company, Pay Your Family First, and began creating experiential and affordable products originally aimed for young adults...coming full circle to where my true passion had started with my son's trouble years earlier. In creating these products, it felt like a direct download from my own life of experience...and it was a great relief!

Then, just a few months later, I received a call from the White House inviting me to join the first President's Advisory Council on Financial Literacy. I had the honor of serving our President...but more important, it gave me a national voice that allowed me to highlight the importance of financial and entrepreneurship education.

And then another call came in...and it was from the Napoleon Hill Foundation. My husband and I had known Don Green for several years and had great respect for his leadership in keeping the works and wisdom of Napoleon Hill alive around the world. I had first read Hill's most famous work, *Think and Grow Rich*, when I was 19 years old and didn't realize the impact it had on me...until that call. It was March 20, 2008, when Don Green called and asked me to step into a project called *Three Feet From Gold*. I was speechless, but quickly responded with, "Absolutely!" It felt like I had been invited home because my passion and mission were so aligned with those of the Foundation. Have you ever had the feeling that the stars were aligned in your own life? I did at that moment.

Greg Reid and I went on to co-author *Three Feet From Gold*, which highlights Hill's philosophy of perseverance and "never giving up." We interviewed 35 of today's successful leaders about not just their success stories, but how they made it through the darkest times and persevered to build their great successes. It reveals the power of association. The month we released the book in 2009, I had two additional calls that became new "turning points" for me, one from the American Society of Certified Public Accountants and another call from Don Green.

It seemed my career had come full circle in its twilight, as the AICPA asked me to join their National CPAs Financial Literacy Commission to serve as a national spokesperson to promote financial literacy. It is an incredible honor to serve as a spokesperson, and they have now asked me to serve as the editor of the AICPA's first mass market book on financial education to be released in celebration of its 125th anniversary in 2012.

The call from Don Green in 2009 was equally life-changing. He asked me to review a newly discovered manuscript that Napoleon Hill had written in 1938, just after he published *Think and Grow Rich*, the bestselling personal development and business book of all time. He had titled the manuscript *Outwitting the Devil* and had intended it to be published as the sequel to *Think and Grow Rich*. However, the manuscript scared Hill's wife and she forbade it from being published. It had been hidden for over 70 years. As I read it, it was as if Napoleon Hill was speaking directly to me. Even though it was written so long ago, it is a perfect message for people struggling during today's difficult economic times.

At the time he wrote it, Hill had become frustrated by the realization that even though people would read and learn the steps to becoming successful from *Think and Grow Rich*, many of them would still not reach the level of success they truly deserved. He wrote *Outwitting the Devil* in the hope that it would help people break through their fears and get past the self-limiting beliefs that were holding them back.

I believe the book being hidden for so many years served a higher and greater purpose. So many people today are paralyzed by fear, unable to deal with the economic troubles from the past few years. *Outwitting the Devil* may just be the right book at the right time. One reviewer wrote, "*Outwitting the Devil* will create a cosmic shift in positive outcomes."

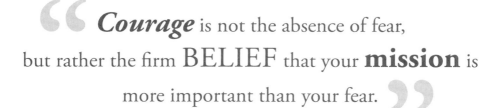

> *Courage* is not the absence of fear, but rather the firm BELIEF that your **mission** is more important than your fear.

In working on the book, which was published in June of 2011, I truly felt at peace. The book helped me understand how fear had really held me back in my own life so many times, and yet it also showed me how I had been able to conquer that fear along the way. It brought true clarity behind my mantra of "Why Not?" When you live in fear, you live in a state of asking the question, "Why?" It gives you an excuse for not moving forward. It may prevent you from realizing your dreams. This fear is crippling, and as Hill reveals, it is the number one tool of a manmade devil.

In contrast, when you ask yourself, "Why Not?," you are charting a new course, you are stepping outside the box, and you are revealing the unknown with eager anticipation of what the future may hold. You are challenging the status quo and eagerly seeking the unknown. All of these are traits of a true entrepreneur.

Every decision you make, every phone call you receive, every trauma you experience creates an opportunity for a turning point in your life. May you learn to recognize it, embrace it, step into the unknown and realize all that it has to offer to you.

Instead of asking yourself "Why?"…start asking yourself "Why Not!"

May you be blessed with success. DM

SHARON LECHTER

www.sharonlechter.com
CEO of Pay Your Family First
Annotator of *Outwitting the Devil*
Co-Author of *Three Feet From Gold* and *Rich Dad Poor Dad*

Stroke of Genius

I F YOUR LIFE were a book and you were the author, how would you want your story to read? That's a question that changed my life forever. Great stories have unsuspecting events that change the plot and grip the reader to every page. My life story wasn't a drama or intense action adventure, but it was an amazing life full of love, imagination, great friends, meaningful work, and family.

Turn the page, and a new chapter describes a typical Saturday as my wife, Kim, and I were off to dinner with some friends. During the short drive to the restaurant, I was making a left turn and I suddenly felt like I was going to pass out, thinking *Wow, that was weird, maybe I just need to eat something after an active day of running, swimming, and weight lifting.* The rest of the drive was bizarre because I couldn't feel my right foot on the gas pedal, so I had to gauge my speed by constantly looking at the speedometer. As I got out of the car, I felt disoriented. Never having experienced this before, I simply told Kim I was dizzy and "something is wrong with me." "You'll be fine. When's the last time you ate?" she asked.

Seated at the restaurant, not only could I not remember the last time I ate, but the menu I held in my hands appeared to be written in a language I couldn't understand. On top of that, the vision in my right eye was foggy. *This is so strange,* I thought. *I've never felt anything like this before.* Our friends pulled out a smart phone and Googled my symptoms of "dizzy, numbness, blurred vision on one side." You could tell by their facial expressions that the results didn't match the energetic, young, and physically fit friend that sat across the table.

In a final attempt to evaluate what was really happening to me, I got up from the table and went outside to get some fresh air. After taking a few deep breaths, I looked up toward the sky and experienced a thought for the very first time, "I might die today."

I returned to our table and told Kim we needed to go to the hospital. "Now?" she asked, still thinking I just needed to eat something. After all, I hadn't been to a doctor in years. I wasn't a pound overweight, I exercised every day, and I was the guy others looked up to as an example of health and fitness. I thought I was invincible and figured I'd live past 100.

I explained my symptoms to the lady at the emergency window, and she said, "Don't panic, but this is going to go really fast." For someone who didn't even know what a stroke was, I was surprised when she picked up the intercom and said, "Code stroke." I asked myself, "Is she talking about me? Stroke? Are you kidding me?"

As I was being whisked into the emergency room, my first thoughts were, "How could this be happening? Why me? I'm in great shape; I'm healthy and strong." Then came the exact moment I had to make a defining decision. Needles, machines, and little round stickers with wires were being applied to my body, and I realized I had two choices. I asked myself, "Am I victim lost in a sea of suffering patients at Grossmont Hospital, or can I smile, despite the fear, and be grateful?" For a slight moment, I remember consciously feeling myself going down the victim road. Thankfully, I was able to pull out of the skid and straighten out with a few positive thoughts like,

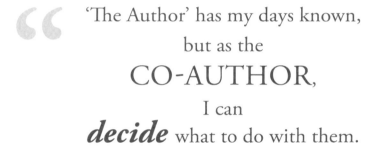

" 'The Author' has my days known,

but as the

CO-AUTHOR,

I can

decide what to do with them. "

"Good thing I am healthy and strong because this incident could have been so much worse," and "Wow, I am so fortunate and lucky!" There are countless stroke patients here that are in much worse condition than I am." This was ***my stroke of genius.*** Every time a negative thought entered my mind, I would turn it around and find a positive thought to replace it.

So If you've just failed your college history exam, turn it around and be thankful that you are part of the 1% of the world's population that has the privilege to attend college. If you didn't care for the roast beef sandwich at lunch today, realize that 95%

of the world's population didn't have any kind of meat today. When work keeps you at the office late and you don't get home until midnight, be thankful for the pillow and blankets that keep you warm and comfortable when you sleep.

Kicking negative thoughts out of your mind takes work! I'm still a work in progress—just ask my own family. When we're watching a San Diego Charger football game and Phillip Rivers throws an interception, I've been known to revert to my days of *"stroke of ignorance"* and count the team up for another loss at half-time. And it's more than just favorite sports teams, it's easy to compare yourself to others and focus on questions like, "Why am I so... unhappy, thin, fat, hairy, bald, short, tall, broke, stupid, geeky, too busy, not busy, focused, unfocused, _____." I bet you can fill in the blank with a word you've thought recently...maybe in the last hour? Regardless, your stroke of genius lies in your ability to detox your mind with positive information. Turn off the news and turn on your iPod to an uplifting story. Turn off your inner heckler and turn on your favorite song that pumps you up and makes you feel vibrant and alive! Turn off your need to be liked by others and turn on your authentic self who pursues your passion.

You can't think negative thoughts while reading or listening to POSITIVE uplifting information. The book you hold in your hands is a perfect example! It's tough to get down in the dumps when you are reading encouraging and uplifting stories.

Back in my younger years, when I'd hit a few night clubs, there would always be at least one huge, intimidating, muscular man with an earpiece and walkie talkie standing at the door. If some joker inside the club did or said something obnoxious or inappropriate, he got "bounced" out of the place. When your inner heckler states something negative like, "You suck, you're too young, old, dumb, etc.," you need to be the bouncer of your own mind. Simply demand those thoughts to "expose themselves." Ask them, "Who are you? Where did you come from? Come into the light. You are not welcome here any longer, so long chump!"

Writing this unsuspecting chapter in my life made me realize for the first time that I was not the author or controller of my life—I was the co-author. For the first time, I experienced a realization that "I'm really not in control of how many days I will have." 'The Author' has my days known, but as the co-author, I can decide what to do with them. I became liberated with this new realization! Wow! I get to decide how much passion, happiness, and gratitude I can juice from today. From the emergency room until today, I have not let a day pass without realizing each day is a gift. Every morning I wake, I humbly accept a new beautiful box with gorgeous wrapping paper and an elegant bow. Today is a gift, and what I do with it is a gift back to my author and those around me.

You don't need an "emergency room" experience to jolt yourself into a new mindset. All you need is to have the courage to ask and answer this question each day, "What do I REALLY want to be doing with my life?" And each day, make another step forward to your answer. When your inner heckler tries to derail you or a doubting thought leaps into your mind, remember your stroke of genius, "What's something good I can replace this with?"

Humans are unique because we are the only species who can completely change the course of our thinking, and thus our lives—lizards can't do it, and neither can alligators or lions. If a goose wanted to fly west instead of south for the winter, it couldn't. All other animals besides humans are directed entirely by the impulses of their genetic code. As a human, if you don't like the story of your life thus far, you can rip up the script and write a completely new one. Ask anyone who has achieved great success in life if there was a turning point, perhaps an "emergency room" experience where they made a clear and resolute decision that, from that moment forward, their life would never be the same.

The collection of stories you hold in your hands are all living proof of these defining decisions. Story after story, someone drew a figurative line in the sand and created a new vision of themselves and the life they were committed to living. Some make that turning point at the age of 15, some not until they are 50. Some do it several times throughout their lives, and some never at all. My question for you is, "Is right NOW your turning point?" Consider that what you have accomplished thus far is only a fraction of what's truly possible for you. You are far more powerful, capable, and gifted than you have allowed yourself to be. The only thing separating you from the grandest vision of your life is COURAGE. Muster the courage to declare that right now, this day, can be your turning point.

I read a story recently about a man in his late 80s who was asked a sobering question. "If you could come back and live the life of anybody you wanted, who would it be?" His answer was so revealing about how most of us live our lives: "I would want to come back as the man I could have been, but never was." He said, "This time I would act with more courage, I wouldn't allow my fear to turn me away from opportunities I didn't take, I'd risk more, I'd take more chances, I'd allow myself to fail more, love more and laugh more, this time I'd be sure to *live* more."

It might be too late for him, but it isn't too late for you. If you're really committed to becoming financially secure, getting healthy, improving your marriage, or being a person of character that your children, colleagues, and the community can look up to, then it's time to grow up and do something about it. Make a decision to take control of your thoughts and happiness. Your stroke of genius awaits! DM

BRAD DeHAVEN

 Muster the courage to declare
that right now,
this day,
can be your turning point.

BRAD DeHAVEN

Impossibility

M OST OF THE stories in this book talk about how people reached their defining moment. This one talks about how you can become a defining moment, both for yourself and for others. And it's a story that starts almost 50 years ago—a story, that in the 1960's, was an important, world-changing event. You might be thinking that this story, which took place in September of 1964, may have had something to do with the civil rights movement, JFK's assassination, Vietnam, flower power, or the beginning of the race to put a man on the moon. All of those stories are much more famous. But what this story lacks in fame, it makes up for in change-the-world impact—at least the world for a kid named James.

This story takes place in Most Precious Blood, an elementary school in Denver, Colorado. (Yes, that's really its name.) It involves a sixth-grade teacher by the name of Amy Thompson, and it started the month before school was set to begin. Miss Thompson was reviewing the students in her new class with Sister Immaculata (yes, that was really her name, too), who had taught the fifth grade the previous year. They went over each and every student, reviewing their strengths and where they needed help. They were almost finished with the review when Amy came across a kid who was a problem, and seemed to have lots of problems. This kid's name was James, and his fifth grade year was, by all accounts, a disaster. His grades had dropped dramatically from fourth grade. He was kept after school as often as he was able to go home on time. He was in fights on the playground, and, because he was a big kid, he wasn't scared of fighting the sixth, seventh, or eighth graders. That usually didn't turn out very well for anyone. He had hardly any friends, and he was constantly made fun of by most of his classmates.

You see, James was an epileptic, and as such, his actions were unpredictable and sometimes even scary. There's a reason, in times past, that epileptics were treated like lepers and put on their own, isolated colonies. They were thought to be possessed. His staring spells were weird. His occasional loss of bodily functions was disconcerting. His anger at the constant teasing of his schoolmates was scary. Spaz. Weirdo. Freak. Those were his nicknames. He was a lost kid and in a downward spiral.

Now, Most Precious Blood was a Catholic school of ordinary means. Their teachers were paid less than their public school counterparts. There were no special ed teachers to help with James or no teacher's assistants to help distract him. And usually, at Most Precious Blood, the involvement of parents was a good thing—except in this case. Parents were fearful and angry based on the wild "James stories" their sons and daughters would tell at the dinner table. They had become upset with the school for not stepping in more forcefully.

So what was Miss Thompson going to do? She had 30 other kids to teach that year and 60 other parents who didn't want a repeat of the previous year's classroom disruption.

The school wasn't going to solve the problem with some new program, some new person. What was she going to do about James? Well, here's what she did. On the first day, she asked James to stay after class. He thought, "Here we go again. This is just great." But instead of being in trouble, Miss Thompson sat down with the young and confused kid and said, "James, I know last year was hell. I know all of the things that happened to you and your reaction to them. I think I would have had the same reaction if I was in your situation. But I also know you have a special talent, especially in writing. And that's going to be the key to making your sixth grade year different than your fifth grade year. I want you to know it's not going to be like it was last year, and I'm going to help make sure of that. We'll stay after school, but not because you're in trouble, but because I want to bring out this wonderful talent that you have. And by the end of this year, everyone will see you in a new light. That is, if that's what you want."

" Most of the stories in this book talk about how people reached their defining moment.

This one talks about how you can become a *defining moment*, both for YOURSELF and for OTHERS. "

Well, James couldn't turn that down. He was lost and scared, but he knew a good thing when he heard it. After all, he didn't want to be a spaz or a freak. He wanted to go back to being a kid of recognized talent—a kid that fit in, a kid that had friends, a kid that had a future. So that year, Miss Thompson and James worked together. And, little by little, the talent and confidence grew. His writing became as important to his "recovery" as the combination of medicines that finally controlled his seizures.

If you fast forward this story a little bit, it has quite an ending. James's grades from seventh grade through high school were A's. He got an academic scholarship to high school. He became a big-time high school athlete and valedictorian of his class. He got scholarships to every college he applied to, and he went to Notre Dame. He got a Master's Degree and went on to be a consultant, an author, a public speaker, and an entrepreneur. He started three successful companies, two of them listed in the Inc. 500 fastest growing private companies in the U. S. James' world had changed as dramatically as any world could. The impossible had happened for him, and all because of a personal decision Amy Thompson made. She decided that *she* could be a defining moment for James. She didn't wait for someone else to do it. She didn't think the answer was in her school. Amy Thompson took a hopeless and sometimes scary kid, and she inspired him. She guided him. She transformed him. I should know. My middle name is James. I was that kid.

I tell you this story for three big reasons. First, it's an important story to me, and by telling it, I get to spend some time with Miss Thompson and let you know what a remarkable person she was. I always like that. Second, it gives me an opportunity to open your eyes to something very special. I want you to think back to your Miss

Thompson. Think about the person who believed in you more than you believed in yourself. Who came along just at the right time and just in the right circumstance—the person who saw something in you that was wondrous and helped you bring it out? When you think of that time in your life, wouldn't it qualify as a defining moment?

That brings us to the third reason I told you that story. While many times a defining moment is a circumstance, a realization, or a decision—it can also be a person. You can be a defining moment for someone else. Just think back to your mentor and what he or she saw in you and did about it. What if you decided, on an everyday basis, that you would do that for others—that you would be the turning point, the defining moment in their lives? Think of the change that you could make. Think of what could be possible. Think of how many defining moments you could create. Since Miss Thompson helped me, I've been able to do the same thing for lots of people, and there's nothing that is more important, or more rewarding than that. As a matter of fact, I think if I were to write on my tombstone, it would read something like: "He helped people do what they thought was impossible."

Now, I know you might be thinking, "Can I really do all of that? After all, I've got challenges and problems of my own and things in my life that need figured out. Who am I to think that I could make a difference in the lives of others? Who am I to help them take on what seems to be impossible circumstances? I'm so small, and that's so big." I understand. I'm sure Amy also had lots of things going on in her life that she didn't figure out before helping this lost kid. I know that I am still very much a work in progress, but I also know that I have been able to help. You can, too.

I'll leave you with this thought. Even though you might feel small, you could have a big effect. Think of that tiny piece of punctuation—the apostrophe. It is small, insignificant, and often misused. And yet, it has a transformational power to it. Look at the word IMPOSSIBILITY. It's a huge word. It's a daunting word. It's a discouraging word. Yet, if you drop in the tiny apostrophe, in just the right place between the I and the M, suddenly it is transformed to I'MPOSSIBILITY. That's what you could do. You could be someone's apostrophe. You could be someone's defining moment. And you can do it today. Amy Thompson made that choice in 1964—she changed my life. I hope you make that choice today. Be a defining moment, don't just wait to have one. DM

GARY ADAMSON

> *Think of how many*
> *defining moments*
> *you could be a part of.*

GARY ADAMSON

Courage, Conscience & Character

M Y DEFINING MOMENT came without warning. While it was delivered by an unlikely messenger, the message was immediately apparent.

I was living in Maui at the time, dating an extremely jealous guy. Truth be told, it wasn't a healthy relationship, although we had some fun times. We fought all of the time. I took a reprieve from our constant arguments and left for a few days to visit a friend who lived on a different island. Relaxing, I picked up a book entitled *How Could You Do That?* by Dr. Laura Schlessinger. While I was reading about the less than desirable choices people make and the consequences that result from them, my defining moment popped off the page and into my head. I wondered, *Why am I with this guy? I need to get the courage to get out of this relationship.* Suddenly, I realized that staying in an unhealthy relationship was my choice, albeit a poor one, but I also had the power to choose differently.

That revelation changed my life. Ending the relationship was my first order of business and one that I embarked on immediately. I approached my boyfriend and explained that I couldn't be the person he needed or wanted. In fact, that was the reason we constantly argued—we were not right for each other and no amount of arguing would ever change that. It was time to stop the madness.

I'd found the courage to end an unhealthy relationship that created turmoil, stress, and unhappiness in both of our lives.

> " I wondered,
> *If courage could change my mindset so significantly, what would happen if I concentrated on all of the three C's of success:*
>
> ## COURAGE, CONSCIENCE & CHARACTER?
>
> Fuelled by curiosity, I was determined to find out. "

A few days later, he returned, begging me to give our relationship a chance. I could have succumbed to my emotions, allowing his pleas and the very real sympathy I felt for him to influence my decision. But, again, I dug deep and found the courage to do what I knew in my heart was right for me. Knowing we weren't right for each other and never would be, I stood by my decision.

Having the courage to break up with him was freeing. The self-imposed limitations I'd placed before myself were gone, and without the barriers, I suddenly was able to see the many possibilities that my newfound courage was eager to explore.

I wondered, *If courage could change my mindset so significantly, what would happen if I concentrated on all of the three C's of success: Courage, Conscience and Character?* Fueled by curiosity, I was determined to find out.

As I thought about my conscience and character, I realized that all of the three Cs affected my life. I was what some might politely call a rebellious teenager. Admittedly, I was not the most stellar member of society. In that moment, I came to the conclusion that I would never make anything of myself if I continued on the path I'd chosen. Resolving to focus on the three Cs, I started my quest to be the best that I could be.

This took some work because I'd made poor choices and displayed bad behavior during my teen years. People already had me labeled because of my previous actions. In other words, I had a reputation. I knew it would take some time for people to see me differently and to trust me again, but it wasn't about them or what they thought— it was about me and what I wanted for my life. Following the three C's not only transformed me, but it also saved me. You see as a teenager, I smoked and experimented with drugs. I defied the law a time or two, as well. If I hadn't read one book or had the courage to make one life-changing decision, I wouldn't have turned my life around.

I quit smoking and doing drugs. In my 20's, I followed a new, healthier path. Not only did I become more conscious of the foods I ate, striving to make healthy, wholesome choices, I made a concerted effort to focus on improving my body and overall fitness.

That journey awakened new interests and achievements as I worked toward earning my Black Belt in Tae Kwon-Do.

While my health and relationships visibly improved, I also turned my attention to my finances, something which I'd neglected. I worked and set goals, saving my money for them. Financial independence led to independence in all areas of life. I found the courage to travel by myself to Spain, to go to a school so I could learn the Spanish language. The world was my oyster, and I explored the options before me. Finally, I decided to move to Vancouver, where I wanted to settle down and enjoy a career as a makeup artist.

But my story doesn't stop there. In fact, that's where it truly began. Over the next decade, I worked alongside my father to bring Quizno's Subs into Canada and oversaw the franchise as it grew to include over 250 stores. Today, I'm in my 30's, retired from my positions as Vice President of Operations for Quizno's and Director of Operations of Southern California from Taco Bell. My courage, conscience, and character have brought me full circle, and now I share my passions to touch, inspire, and empower others. This is, undoubtedly, the most rewarding thing I've ever done—to be passionate about my work and my purpose is the most fulfilling part of any success.

Since my defining moment, I've realized that opportunities are everywhere. In fact, life is an opportunity, one which can produce amazing results if you have the courage, conscience and character to pursue them. I know from experience that success and happiness are within everyone's grasp. No matter what you're going through in life, you deserve and can create a better future. You deserve to have many defining moments. By taking responsibility for your actions in order to make different choices, you have the power to become who you want to be, do what you want to do, and live the life you've always wanted. The biggest obstacle in your path isn't your boyfriend, job, or money—it's you.

I'm proof that anything is possible…if you have the courage to go for it. DM

HEATHER BLAISE

 By taking **responsibility** for your actions in
order to make different choices,
you have the POWER to become who you want to be,
do what you want to do,
and *live the life* you've always wanted.

HEATHER BLAISE

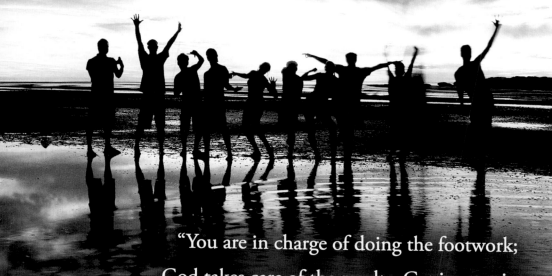

"You are in charge of doing the footwork;
God takes care of the results. Get into action.

Get out of results."

MIKE SOMERVILLE

Surrender. Succeed. Win.

I RAN OUT OF COCAINE very early Monday morning, Memorial Day, May 25, 1992. If someone had said the previous Friday, "*Mikes, you will do your last line of cocaine and drink your last glass of Southern Comfort this weekend,*" I would have told them, "Screw you! I'm going to do coke as often as I can and die by the time I am 30."

It's good to have goals. It's good to have a vision. They describe what the mountaintop will look like and feel like when you "have arrived." At the age of 24, having used cocaine for about three years straight, it really seemed like a good goal to continue drinking, using drugs, and lying, and then kill myself at the age of 30. This is just an example of the way I brainstormed—which can be a downfall for many, but has proven to be my driving force.

The first time I drank alcohol, the first time I saw a girl naked (up close), the day I graduated with a Bachelors degree in electrical engineering (whew! I was done with 50 to 60 hours of homework per week!), my first trip to Duns River Falls in Jamaica, my first drug-free spiritual experience, and the first time I ate a piece of homemade banana bread from Julia's as I traveled up the Honoapilani Highway—these are all thoughts that float/buzz/rattle around in my wonderful, God-given supercomputer: my brain. When I am feeling creative, I refer to this as **brainstorming**. When I am honest enough with myself to acknowledge that I am procrastinating, I call it screwing around. Mix the two together and some might say, "*Mikes, you've got life balance.*" Balance bores me. I believe in living on the edge, giving 110% at 80 miles per hour. However, I admit there were times I took that to extremes—after all, I had preplanned my death at the age of 30! However, I believe that life is not a dress rehearsal…even though I had rehearsed the scene that was being played out on this particular Memorial Day more often than I care to count.

I had run out of cocaine many times—it's not like I ever stopped before I ran out—I mean c'mon, let's face it, if I could use cocaine "normally"… well, shit, I'd use it every day, all day… for the rest of my life. Oh, and an important thing about this fantasy is that neither I nor the loving friends and family that God has blessed me with would experience any negative consequences as a result of my drinking, using and lying. Reality Check: Fat chance! The sober, loving, caring people around me experienced more emotional disappointment watching me bottom out than I probably did while "numb" from chemicals.

I'm a run-of-the-mill addict and alcoholic, which is totally sweet because the 12 step programs work real well when you:

- do what is suggested by the 12 steps;
- seek the guidance of a spiritual guide and mentor for the journey through the steps; (We call those sponsors. I call mine Bill.)
- aren't a self-proclaimed intellectual and spiritual giant whose behavior while drinking and using, or even while sober, makes you somehow terminally unique;
- surrender.

After I ran out, I took a handful of sleeping pills, finished off the Southern Comfort I had in my apartment, and then passed out.

I woke up about 1:30 p.m. that Monday. I was so freaking pissed that I had not been able to just fall asleep and die. As I relive that day in my mind, I'm pretty damn grateful that God had other plans. Nice work, God. I owe you a smoothie!

When I ran out, naturally, I called my dealer. I called him that afternoon and got his voicemail. BASTARD! Every time my dealer answered the phone, he was my best friend. Every time my calls went to voicemail, I freaking hated that guy and said to myself, "*Dude, I gotta get a more responsive connect… one that maybe even delivers…*" Brainstorm!

One of the very famous commercials on late-night TV at that time (shocker that I'd be watching TV in the middle of the night) was the 1-800-COCAINE commercial: "This is drugs; this is your brain on drugs… any questions…" Google it. The message is true—even if you hate fried eggs.

I called that number and even though I could barely speak (when using coke, I would chew on the back of my tongue for hours, so it would swell up and I'd sound like a person with… well… a swollen tongue), the guy on the other end of the line, who was a recovering addict, somehow understood when I mumbled, "I think I have a serious cocaine problem, and I need help." I was expecting him to say, "No problem, sir, for $25,000 you can come to our treatment center for 28 days and we will help you with your problem."

To which I would had answered, "*Dude... If I had $25,000 I would **not** have a cocaine problem, I would have an inventory management/supply-chain management problem...*" I'd explored some treatment programs before and made the executive business decision that it was more fiscally responsible for me to use cocaine—buying it in $1,500/week increments—than it would be to spend $25,000 for treatment... Brainstorm.

> " This was far from a shining moment,
>
> but the humiliation that I felt was definitely
>
> one of the more
>
> **defining moments** of my life. "

To my amazement and pleasure, the guy on the other end could totally relate to my situation. He had been there and he told me how he was able to get sober. I've never forgotten that guy. I've never used cocaine again, either... I owe you more than a smoothie, God.

Next, I called my girlfriend. She and I hadn't really spoken for a few days... or weeks... that part is kind of blurry. She was surprisingly happy to hear from me. I believe the constantly blinking light on my answering machine had some correlation between her need to know if I was okay and my lack of communication with non-cocaine producing humans... I basically had no use for people who could not procure me blow... until now.

I said, *"I've had a pretty bad night* (my "nights" lasted anywhere from 12 to 36 hours… sigh), *and I'm wondering if you can come over."*
"Sure. Can I get you anything?"
"Yeah, I'm out of smokes. Can you pick me up a pack?"
"Sure. I'll come on over."
"Cool. Oh, yeah, while you're at it can you pick me up a bottle of Southern Comfort?"
"ummm… (pause) Okay…"

When she arrived, I had forgotten (or was numb to the fact) that I was naked, sweating profusely, and had Mexican blankets pinned up on my walls, covering up the windows— mainly because my version of "partying" by this time was:

- buy as much cocaine as I could afford
- come back to my studio apartment
- cover up all the windows
- crawl around on the ground, naked, sweating, talking to bugs…

Brainstorm!

She entered, I grabbed the bottle of SoCo from her hands, opened the top and chugged it like it was Evian. After gulping for about 20 seconds (and almost finishing the bottle), I wiped the little dribbles off of my mouth and face with my sweaty right wrist. I looked straight ahead and saw this poor girl's eyes open quite wide, with a look of disappointment, sadness, fear, concern… I'm sure she was wondering, *what the heck do I do with this freak of a boyfriend I have… ugh…*

This was far from a shining moment, but the humiliation that I felt was definitely one of the more **defining** moments of my life.

I ended up passing out at her apartment for about 3 days and then on Thursday, May 28, 1992 at 6:30 p.m., I went to my first 12-step meeting. I have not had a drink or drug (any mind-altering substance that affects me from the neck up) since that day.

Gratitude. Surrender.

Upon arriving at my first meeting, I sat in the front row. When they asked if there were any newcomers present, I raised my hand and said, "*Hi, my name is Mike, and I'm a cocaine addict, and this is meeting one, and I have about a million left to go…*"

Hey God, I'm very clear that you put those words in my mouth that day. Thanks. I owe you a smoothie.

The next seven years of my life, I was very engaged in my recovery… being in recovery is an additional level of spiritual consciousness from being just physically "sober." To me, it means that I get to feel free. I am able to give back to others. By sharing my experience, strength, and hope with others, I get to stay sober one more day—for another 24 hours. And thus I recover. I *get* to go to work today, to pay my taxes, to feel sadness, as well as joy, in the extreme… AMAZING!

From about 2000 to 2002, I did not take care of myself. I share this with you because whether you are an addict, an alcoholic or a "normie," I believe it is crucial to take care of yourself. Whatever that looks like, define it for yourself. Architect the life you have always dreamed about living. You are in charge of doing the footwork; God takes care of the results. Get into action. Get out of results.

In February of 2002, I had an attractive girlfriend, a house in San Diego, a Range Rover, a Rolls Royce (it was my "British car period"), another German convertible, and two houses in Mexico. I was making a six-figure income. For the life of me, I could not buy myself happy. I was miserable. I was **not** living the dream! I was doing it **wrong**. I didn't have a spiritual connection and was eating like crap. On top of that, I was smoking about two packs of non-filtered cigarettes a day and working 12 to 14 hour days. Even worse, I was not attending 12-step meetings. I didn't have a sponsor. I didn't have a coach. I also wasn't praying every morning for guidance or thanking a Higher Power at the end of the day for the wonderful experience(s) I **got** to enjoy during the previous 24 hours. I was a horrible employee. I was a horrible boss. I was broken.

My best (or worst) thinking resulted in me sitting on my girlfriend's bed, holding her unloaded 9mm Glock handgun. I put it up to my lips. To this day, I can still taste the oil smell... the "gun" taste of it.

Of all the experiences I have had in my life, be them ***defining*** or *refining* moments, that is one that I wish I could delete from the database. It sucked. I pray you never get to a point where you think "offing" yourself is the best solution.

Brainstorm… C'mon! That's a Brain Typhoon. Breathe…

This voice in my head said, "This is not a good idea…" YA THINK!!!???

I put down the gun and got up. Grabbing my bag, I walked downstairs and said goodbye to my girlfriend's son, who was in the kitchen. Then I told my girlfriend, "I'm done."

** Here's an important safety tip: Don't date girls who have to carry hand guns because their ex's are on America's Most Wanted… Just sayin…

This was also a time in my life when I looked at the people who I had surrounded myself with and realized that I was not choosing the healthiest 'teammates'… Indeed, I needed a Brain Washing—no more Storming.

I spent the next few years of my life trying to get back to a spot where I would be comfortable in my own skin. I was really freaking lost.

I got back to the basics of reaching out to people and asking for help. I got a sponsor and started going to meetings regularly… daily… twice a day. I also regained a connection with a Higher Power, who I reach out to in different ways today. Praying has become my new norm—I pray on my knees and while walking or standing at the urinal or in the car. I pray before going on that really scary ride at the Del Mar Fair where you free fall 100 feet and get such an adrenaline rush that you shake after it stops at the bottom. Sometimes I pray that one ride on it will be enough. It rarely is. I pray at both weddings and funerals. I pray at the

beach. I pray with my girlfriend. I hold the hand of another brother who is on a journey that he finds very uncomfortable and share my stories with him, hoping it helps them be grateful for all the imperfections in their life that are "big deals" or "complicated"… Life is a gift… Bring it!

Have you ever responded to a friend or loved one who genuinely asks, "How are you?" with "It's complicated, you wouldn't understand?" THAT's BULL! It's only complicated because you are making it that way. Stop that. Make a ***defining moment*** in your life and the life of your trusted friend by taking the negative energy out of this "too complicated" situation.

Call your best friend, right now, and share this!
Tell them they are AMAZING. If you can't do that with your best friend, get a new one.

Call your mentor, right now! Tell them how important they are in your life.
(As I was writing this, I thought to myself, 'I wonder if anyone will really do this? I hope they do. That would be a wonderful thing for you and the recipient. So, I put down my laptop for all of three minutes and called my sponsor and mentor, Bill.)

If I ever have the pleasure of meeting you one day, you may assess that I am quite lively, sometimes very lively. I'm also animated and speak quite quickly. You might even say, "Mikes, are you clean and sober for 19 years or have you been using for 19 years?" HAH! I am VERY happy – passionate about topics that involve helping others help themselves. Today, I'm naturally "caffeinated" and have a passion for life that frequently exceeds my expectations. I am in love with me… all of me… with all of my self-judged imperfections.

I bet God thinks everything about me is perfect!

If I can live the dream, so can you. Remember, I'm nothing special—just a precious child of God doing the best that I can with the level of awareness that I have at this very moment. I am no better and no worse than you.

Do it.

Surrender. Succeed. Win.
Live the Dream!
If you're not, you're doing it wrong.
I have no right to be here if I'm not adding value. I would be honored to add value to your life if I may. Let me know how I can help.
Define the next moments of your life. Architect them. Live the Dream!

Ask for help. Send me an e-mail letting me know how I can help you or sharing how you Live the Dream:

info@AmazingLife.us

Lemme know how it goes. DM

MIKE SOMERVILLE

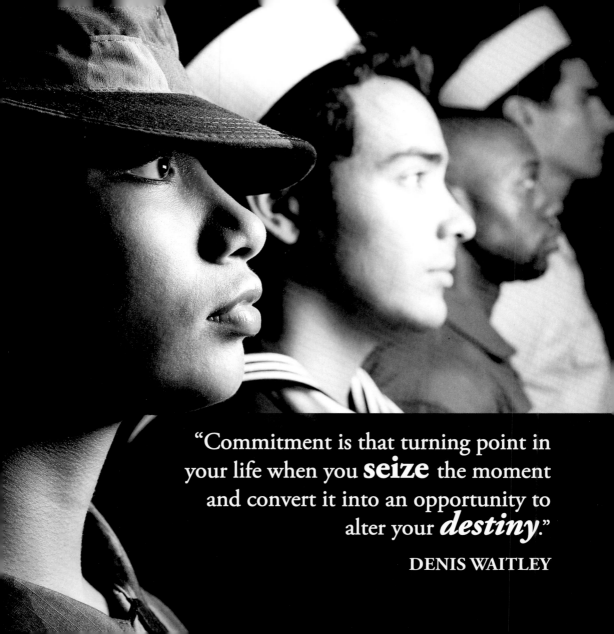

"Commitment is that turning point in your life when you **seize** the moment and convert it into an opportunity to alter your *destiny*."

DENIS WAITLEY

BECOMING ONE OF THE
Few and Proud

IT WAS A COLD October day when I was smacked by the reality of growing up. A 17-year-old senior in high school, I walked into the Audubon Green Wave football locker room to get ready for practice. My mind was introduced to the opportunity of traveling the world, creating a name for myself, and serving my country by joining the United States Armed Forces. Suddenly, the childish games and fun came to a screeching halt, and the echo of "what am I going to do with my life" became so loud in the walls of my mind. As I looked around at my peers, I found that many of them were already halfway down the road, figuring out what college they wanted to go to, busily applying and receiving acceptance letters. The thought of playing sports in college was a dream since childhood, but I quickly realized that life's not fair and college sports were on a level that my talent didn't quite meet. My whole world seemed to be getting smaller and smaller, along with the opportunities to make something of myself and prove to my family and friends that I was a "somebody" that was going to make a positive impact on the world.

Days and weeks went by, and the holidays were approaching. I didn't want to be the outcast among all my friends, who were celebrating, one by one, the success of taking the first steps toward the rest of their life. Other than a community college, I knew college was not an option, and the thought of piling up student loans was not too galvanic for me. My options were limited, and my defining moment was approaching. I knew I was at a fork in the road in life—was I to go down the road to start my working career or take the path of the United States Armed Forces?

During the next few days, my mind housed a mental tornado. My focus was now dialed in on the rest of my life. Input from family and friends was no use; it came and went like a feather in the wind. I knew it was going to be my decision only.

If I was to go down the road to start my working career, I knew it would be tough. It would mean early rises and long days, for there are not that many opportunities for an 18-year-old kid to get ahead in today's generation. I didn't know what to do as a profession, and living at home was not an option anymore. I became a financial burden in my house as times were tough, and I knew I had to leave the nest in order to conquer the world. Suddenly, the option of serving my country was more and more appealing, like an ice cream cone on a hot summer day. The Armed Forces was making more sense, especially since both my grandfathers served: one in the Army in the Vietnam War and the other in the Navy in WWII.

I started doing research on all the branches of the services. In the tenth grade, my anatomy teacher brought his brother, a dentist in the Navy, in to speak to our class. He made the Navy ship life sound so exciting as he shared slideshows and stories of the diverse cultures around the world. So that was first on my list to check out. The Army was not appealing to me, and the Air Force seemed like it wouldn't challenge my active lifestyle, simply put.

As I was doing my research, one of my older buddies returned from the Iraq War and visited our school. He was dressed in a uniform I had never seen before. He wore a dark black jacket with gold buttons that shone like the twinkling of the stars, and the chevrons were perfectly centered on his sleeves, while the collar was snuggling his neck. He wore solid blue, perfectly pressed pants with a red stripe that went down the sides, and held a just as perfect white cover at a 90-degree angle in his arm. His shiny black shoes glared at me so much I could see myself in them. I had never heard of this branch before, but I quickly learned about the United States Marine Corps. His recruiter was with him and did not miss a beat. He was throwing his pitch about the Marine Corps, but it was the uniform and the stories about Iraq that had me dazed. My emotions were high and buried deep within me because 9/11 took place the previous year. Instantly, I knew where my future was headed. And because I was still three months from turning 18, I knew I would need my parents' permission to join any branch of the military.

That evening, I quickly ran home to celebrate the victory of finding my defining moment with my mother. To my disappointment, as the words rolled out my mouth at jet speed, she was unhappy. She filled me in that the Marines were the first to fight; they went to the front lines of the battlefield and to the brunt of the battles. Her words were disheartening, but I was still sold. Days of verbal battle went back and forth between family and friends. My grandfather tried to tell me how safe the Air Force was, but that was just not where I saw the warrior spirit within me being utilized. I would not give up on defending this unofficial partnership that I had for the Marines. As talks continued, people gave valid points, but I stood my ground on the fact the Marines have the best training and would have the best chances of survival.

A week later, in early November, we came to an agreement in the best way to decide whether I would enter the Navy or United States Marine Corps. I struck a deal with my mother that I would listen to a Navy recruiter with her if she would listen to my Marine recruiter with me. Then we could balance our options and make a collective decision, although secretly I knew my decision.

The next day, I asked my football coach to allow me to skip practice on Wednesday so I could see both recruiters. As he granted me the permission, I had my foot halfway out the door to scoop my mother up and head to the recruiters.

First was the Navy; they were long, drawn out, and didn't fit the part of a fit military personnel. In my head, I knew they were not the service for me, and I was role playing in my mind how my Marine recruiter would win my mother over, and I would be off to see the world from there.

As we left, I knew she wasn't completely sold, either, as she tried to draw out my feelings from the meeting. But it was no use; my mind was locked in on the Marine meeting, like a sniper focused on his target. That night my Recruiter did his magic, and being a mother, she could see that this was what I really wanted in my life. We left that office both fully sold, and I was ready to commit to becoming a United States Marine.

After weeks of paperwork and physicals, it was time to sign the next five years of my life away—except there was one hold up: my mother wouldn't sign if I was to be a grunt. My heart took a wound, but I was determined to join, so I took the M.O.S. of an Aviation Electronics Technician. On November 22, 2002, I was opted in to the United States Marine Corps Depot Program. I had the option to leave in September after spending my senior summer parting with friends and saying my goodbyes, or I could leave ten days after graduation on June 30, 2003. It was another tough decision, but my long-term vision kicked in and I choose option B, ten days after graduation. As the weeks and months rolled by, graduation was approaching fast. The excitement of leaving what I thought was a prison sentence was now becoming the reality of freedom to graduate to "The Real World." As that excitement grew, the sense of fear crept in, too, in leaving for boot camp. A new world, a new life, away from the comfort of friends and family, I knew I would have to stand alone on my own.

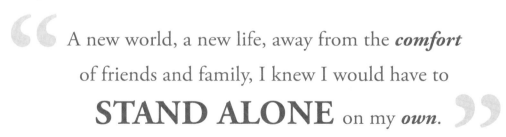

" A new world, a new life, away from the ***comfort*** of friends and family, I knew I would have to **STAND ALONE** on my *own*. "

Graduation day came and went. After months of preparation, work outs, and study sessions, I was excited and nervous about leaving for my new world experience. With 24 hours left of freedom, I helped my mom pack the house up so she could move the next

day to save money and get a grip on her finances. I made a video for all my friends to watch, talking about each of them, one by one, and delivering prior memories and what they each meant in my life.

With my mind racing and emotions stirred up like a crashing wave, I went to bed that night. I awoke the next morning, both excited and nervous. As time drew closer, my friends came to say goodbye and see me off. My mom had to leave to get a moving truck to pack for the next day's move. Moments after she left, my recruiter picked me up. My friends were upset and shocked that I was the first one to leave on my chase toward the future. I handed the tape off to them to watch, and I found out later that they all went inside after I left to watch it and were emotionally touched. The goodbyes to my friends, my home, and my life and comfort zone were now pushed to its limits. It was time for a new life, new adventures, new friends, and experiences. Hours later, I found myself on an airplane for the first time, nervous as can be.

After hours of flying and conquering those fears, I landed in South Carolina. I was quickly shocked to hear yelling right out of the terminal. Walking down the hall, I realized it was a drill instructor who was there to pick us up. We sat for two hours with our heads between our knees before we got any instructions. When we did, we were told we could make one call home to tell our family we made it. It was late in the evening, and my mother didn't answer. I thought to myself, great, she is going to worry for three months now. Luckily, other family answered, promising to relay the message that I would see them next as a United States Marine. We then boarded a bus to Paris Island, South Carolina.

Half in a daze in the dark-tinted bus at whatever time it was, I could smell the hot South Carolina summer night. We pulled in through the guard post, and I knew it was only a matter of time. After a few minutes, the bus came to a halt, the doors opened, and I saw my first real drill instructor. Suddenly, the videos I had watched in my recruiter's office and YouTube instantly become a reality. Instructions were delivered, and we rushed off the bus and found ourselves standing on the famous yellow footprints that constitute that there is no turning back.

Over the next three months, there were extreme lifestyle adjustments, and I had no choice but to adapt to them. Less than eight hours sleep, only three meals a day, early mornings, fire watches, extreme workouts, martial arts, marching, shooting a rifle, no communication with the outside world other than letters, and many other things. But through the hard times and periods of loneliness, I always kept in the forefront of my mind the reason I was doing this and who I was doing it for. I can remember marching on the parade deck as the sun would set on those hot summer days, picturing my family in the stands watching me graduate. That is what kept me going in those moments that I wanted to give up and didn't think I could keep going. But after three months of discovering what I could really accomplish if I focused my mind to it, I finally was ready to graduate.

I woke up that morning excited to see my family again and to leave this place I now knew as home. We packed our possessions and staged them outside. We got in formation one last time as a platoon and a band of brothers that learned to work as one, regardless of where we all came from. We started marching to the parade deck and could see the ecstatic families in the stands. It was time!

The music was playing, the sun was shining down as if there was a spotlight on myself, and my family was watching in the crowd. The cameras were rolling, and I was standing tall in my green uniform. I stuck my hand out to receive my Eagle, Globe, and Anchor, which signified the right to be called a United States Marine. It was at that time that I knew I had a defining moment in my life, as so many others have traveled the same journey and experienced the same defining moment. DM

JOE MOFFETT

> *People make the mistake of thinking they need the perfect plan.*
>
> *There is no perfect plan.*
>
> *By definition, there can't be, because a plan is not getting there*
> *- it's only your jumping off point.*

JEFF OLSON

"The *yellow brick road* is filled with potholes. However, potholes shouldn't stop you from getting to your destination.

It would be so unfortunate to give up, turn around, and go back, rather than working on filling in those potholes so your journey is a smoother and more enjoyable."

JOHNATHAN PERRYMAN

Defined by Reflection

AS I'M SURE IT IS FOR MANY, my defining moment was also one of my most difficult moments. Maybe that's because when we feel our deepest pain, we are vulnerable, allowing the people, events, and influences that shape us to penetrate the barriers we've built over time. Perhaps, it's when we are at our weakest that we stop trying to define the moments in our lives and let our guard down long enough for a few rare moments to define us.

I got the call in the summer of 2007. On the other end of the line was my brother, Marco, who was crying as his shaking voice broke the news. My voice trembled, as well, and I screamed with all the breath I had left, "No!" when Marco told me that my dad had just had a heart attack and wasn't breathing. I hung up the phone and looked over to Noel, my wife. Immediately, she knew something was wrong—she knew the eyes of desperation and hopelessness. That's when the tears came. I raced to the house where Dad and Marco lived and found the emergency crew trying to revive him. In disbelief, I grabbed Marco and we cried in each other's arms. At 55 years old, our dad had left us. What were we supposed to do now?

Most of that day is still a big blur, as are many of the moments and days that followed. There was so much that had to be taken care of in planning the burial, family gathering, rosary, etc. Of course, as his oldest son, I was involved in making my dad's final arrangements.

I can now appreciate how difficult it is to have to tend to these details while coping with the very fresh grief of a devastating loss. My main focus was getting through the next few days, while keeping busy with the tasks that had been delegated to me. I was responsible for putting together a video montage of all the pictures that our family could find of Dad, and then adding some of his favorite songs to it. The end result would hopefully be a beautiful tribute that would be played at my father's service. As I revisited my dad's life through photos and memories, though, I received my defining moments.

After gathering all the pictures that the family provided, along with three CD's for the musical background, I sat down with a friend from church and we began uploading photos to the video. Each picture produced instant tears. In a certain picture of Dad holding me and my sister, he spoke to me with such a strong look of both love and pain. This moment became particularly unique, however, when I looked into his eyes. It brought me back to that day, and I could remember him hugging us and telling me to "protect your family," "stand up for yourself," and "fight if you have to." At first, this trip back in time brought tears, but then those tears turned into a smile and some laughter. After the emotions settled, though, it seemed that there was another constant that the photo and memories brought me—reflection. Those life lessons that Dad had shared with me were once again in the forefront of my mind, but I realized that they hadn't been for some time. I had gotten pushed off the path and hadn't steered myself back on. I suddenly realized that my dad had left me with so much more than memories and photographs.

I dug a little deeper and came up with a picture I have always loved. There he was, my dad in his prime, dressed in a tux and wearing a black cowboy hat. Dad's thick mustache gave him a presence, and he was looking sharp and in control. Once again, I was drawn back to that day and remembering the scent and the vibe of the afternoon. Dad smelled like a million bucks and looked even better. He strutted around that wedding reception and owned it. He was cool and carried a swag that very few could keep up with. That's just how Dad was. Where was I in this picture? I was right next to him, feeling so proud to be his son. Confidence was one of his very strong points, and that day he demonstrated that quality perfectly. This memory of my dad brought yet another awakening moment. What happened to my swag? For years, I used to carry that same confident swag. When did I lose it? More important, how? Like my dad, my confidence used to be a tank that was always full. Where was it now? As I contemplated those questions, it didn't escape me that this really cool picture had caused me to reflect on another great lesson I'd learned from my dad.

I tried to stay in the moment and disregard all the reflections that were coming my way. At the time, it was too difficult to handle. Staying on task, I pushed through and completed the DVD. The end product is a powerful tribute to my father and something I will have forever. My dad would be proud of me for keeping his spirit alive for all his children.

The church service and DVD tribute were incredible. Being with all of my family members and brothers and sister brought instant tears and emotions that, at times, were really difficult to hide. I keep remembering that at that time, I was at my worst, but I wanted to be strong. Although I'd reviewed the DVD several times, I had promised myself that I was going to smile and enjoy it this time. Fat chance! Every pause between songs was filled with sniffles and tears by everyone around me.

After the service, a celebration of my dad's life was held at my home. The company and food were great. After we'd all gathered for family pictures, the day was finally complete. A nice shower and a much-needed hug from Noel, and I was in bed. Anyone else might have cried themselves to sleep while reflecting on the day; however, my thoughts steered in another direction. *I'm on my own now. It is time to stand up and take a stand.*

> It's when we are at our weakest that we *stop trying* to define the moments in OUR LIVES and let our guard down long enough for a few rare moments to **define us.**

It has been four years since that frightful call from Marco. Four years allows for incredible reflection.

I reflect on all the successes that I attribute to my dad and the things he taught me. With all those wins in my life, it hurts that he's not here to share them with me. However, I do believe he is looking over me and helping me make better choices daily. I've gotten back on the path, with his lessons as my guide:

- **If you want it, you have to work for it**

I was taught to work for things. Hard work is very underrated. Many know this, but simply put, do not apply it.

- **Expect to get beat up a little**

The yellow brick road is filled with potholes. Those potholes are limited belief, lack of knowledge, lack of resources, including money, and they are all legitimate. More often than not, they are viewed as obstacles that prevent you from driving on the road. However, potholes shouldn't stop you from getting to your destination. It would be so unfortunate to give up, turn around, and go back, rather than working on filling in those potholes so your journey is smoother and more enjoyable.

- **Always look good (this is a good one)**

Be proud of who you are. You are a smart, charismatic person that carries yourself in a proud, successful way. You also have a humbleness about you that is very appealing. You embrace success and always remember what hard work feels like. I remember my father looking into the mirror and reminding himself that he looked good. He was teaching me how important it is to embrace positive self-talk.

Positive self-talk is so important. However, it is all too often misconstrued as cocky, arrogant, and conceited. I disagree. I would rather listen as I build myself up, rather than putting myself down. Being my own biggest critic makes no sense to me.

Take that same value of positive self-talk, and now apply it to your young loved ones. In that respect, it doesn't sound very arrogant or cocky. Jordan, my 11-year-old, has been taught from a very young age about the importance of positive self-talk. I once heard her struggling with getting her new contacts into her eyes. After a few tries, she stopped. Before attempting the last time, she looked in the mirror and said to herself, "I can do this. My dad told me I am awesome, and awesome people can do this." And she did do it. That's not conceited; it's very humbling, if you think about it.

- *Never give up*

Simply put, my dad told me that should I ever quit, then I would be a loser. I know it's quite blunt, but yet it is so profound. Without a doubt, it is the absolute 100% truth. Why would one compete if he is just going to quit? Giving up is certain self-defeat, so I choose not to give up. I continue to use this principle in every decision I make today, both personally and with my family.

- *Expect to gain some critics*

I saved this for last because it is my favorite. When you begin an endeavor, whatever that endeavor is, expect someone to criticize you for it. Winners get criticized because they think outside of the box. The glass is always half full with a winner. Believe me when I tell you this—the more critics you have, the better you are doing. Continue to embrace the critics—they help keep the tank on full.

Even with all those lessons my dad left behind, the single most important lesson I learned from my father was to take risks in life. He didn't say it—he lived it. Dad showed me to grab life by the clouds and live it to the fullest. By his model, I learned to take chances and explore what business has to offer. By not restricting myself, I allow doors that open in front of me to swing toward my direction and I'm not reluctant to step in. It was how Dad lived his life, and it has defined my life, as well, as I explore what this great experience called my future has in store for me.

You see, my dad loved to dream. When we were alone, we would talk about boats and dream of different places to visit, like Hawaii, New York, Florida, the Mediterranean, Japan, etc. We even talked about jumping out of a very safe plane into the big blue sky and parachuting down. We joked about what it would feel like and what it would look like. Those precious moments are in the past now, but they will always be remembered.

The DVD I made of my dad's life is one way I can be sure he will always be remembered. It will always be treasured, as will the reflections I received while making it. Creating that tribute was one of my life's defining moments, but the preservation of his influence and the lessons he passed on to me will always define me.

 I can truly say that I am a better man because of my father. The love, encouragement, and wisdom he gave me were exactly what I needed to be the man I am today. DM

JOHNATHAN PERRYMAN

"We have come to understand when
that *moment* comes,
     dare to face the unknown, be *willing* to take the risk,
and *trust* that doing so for the right reasons will allow you
     to take advantage of the *opportunities* presented to you."

RODNEY KESLING

I Want To Be On T.V.

"**I** WANT TO BE ON TV." Cute words coming from a four year old. I suppose many kids that age say such things. At least, that was what my wife and I thought at the time. Lots of kids "play act," doing fun little skits and pretending to be characters they've seen, either in life or on TV. Our daughter was no different—like so many other kids, we believed wanting to be on TV and a fondness for performing was normal at this age. Our daughter, Laura was adorable, and we enjoyed the imagination she showed in her play acting.

Today, my wife, Danielle, and I are sometimes asked what our plan was—but there was no plan. However, there was a mission, although that didn't take hold for a couple more years.

Laura's start in "acting" was completely random. At a motorcycle show in Scottsdale, AZ, we were approached by a lady who commented on how cute Laura was. She asked if we had ever considered putting her in any performing arts classes, such as acting, modeling, or singing. Does anyone's plan for getting their kid started in acting involve attending a motorcycle show? What are the odds? However, because we knew how much fun play acting was for Laura, we engaged the lady in the conversation. She represented a company which specialized in starting kids in performing arts classes, and they had a branch in

Scottsdale. We checked it out and asked Laura if she wanted to try it. My wife and I figured it would be similar to gymnastics or swimming, or any other fun activity that kids might want to try. Her first class wasn't even really acting. It was "Poise and Confidence." She did eventually take some rudimentary acting classes, but those were really just for fun. Laura enjoyed them; however, after a year, her interests were taking her in other directions, and we decided not to continue with the classes and allow her to try other things. Some plan, huh?

Before Laura completely gave up acting, she was invited to participate in an event which the company held each year in Los Angeles. A showcase for young performing talent, it allowed the performers to be seen by industry insiders, such as talent agents, casting agents, and managers. It sounded like fun, and Laura asked to be a part of it, so we decided to make it her "last hurrah" before moving on to other things. The event did involve some performing, so there were a few months of training, practicing, and participating in acting and modeling showcases. Given that some industry insiders were attending the event, everyone knew there was some chance a kid could be "discovered." There were even discussions with the staff regarding expectations for those parents who were concerned with such things. It was reiterated over and over that there were no guarantees, and that any call backs from any talent or casting agent should be considered a success in terms of gaining any recognition. Two or three call backs would be considered huge.

Danielle went with Laura to the two-day event, which was held in early January of 2007 in Century City, near LA. At the time, Laura was six years old. Her performance consisted of a short monologue, a short skit with another kid, and some runway modeling. At the end of the event, Danielle was handed a sheet. Laura had 18 call backs! This was a holy crap moment! Things had now gone from having fun to something more serious. But we had a little problem—we had no clue what to do. It was all so new and foreign to us. The company who staged the event couldn't really help us, and we weren't sure how to proceed on our own.

Luckily, one of the names on the call back list was Susie Mains, a talent manager whom Danielle had met with during the event. They really connected, so Danielle's first instinct was to call Susie for some much-needed advice. Those conversations were a tremendous help. Within two weeks after the showcase event, Laura had a manager and an agent. As we finished signing the contracts with Laura's agent, I asked the obvious question: "What do we do next?" Danielle and I were not prepared for the answer, which was our next "holy crap moment." Laura's agent wanted her in LA, ready to begin taking auditions, by the beginning of February. She'd stay for at least three months—from February through April, which we learned is pilot season in Hollywood. It was January 24th. We were being asked to move from Phoenix to the LA area within two weeks, in the middle of the school year, right when Danielle's golf touring season was beginning, and just as I was starting a new engineering consulting business.

This was our moment. At this point, Danielle and I obviously had to make a choice. "I want to be on TV." Were we prepared to make what was becoming a huge set of sacrifices to enable that dream? Or should we minimize the opportunity and play it safe, rationalizing that it was such a long shot, anyway? What defines us? Personally, I had always been a play-it-safe person. It's not that I didn't try to take advantage of some opportunities in my life, but none were really monumental. I wasn't trained or educated to take the big risk. To the contrary, I was conditioned to minimize risk. Analyze, reduce the unknown, be smart. Play it safe. But this was my daughter—did I really want her to have an opportunity for her dream to happen, and then not allow her to go for it? Would the regret of not trying be heavier than failure? Could I really tell my kids that anything is possible, but not show them how to seize the opportunities presented to them?

> " I was conditioned to minimize risk.
> Analyze, reduce the unknown, be smart.
> # Play it safe.
> But this was my *daughter* - did I really want her
> to have an opportunity for
> ## HER DREAM
> to happen, and then not allow her to go for it? "

There was no plan, but now there was a mission. Enable the dream and allow Laura to pursue her opportunity. We made it work. We split the family. Danielle and my son, Denver, stayed in Phoenix, while Laura and I moved to an apartment in LA for three months. We worked out a program for Laura to stay enrolled in her school, keeping up on her studies through the help of a tutoring program provided by the apartment complex where we lived. We went on auditions nearly every day. There were no guarantees, just a pursuit of the dream. It was exhilarating—tough, and sometimes tedious—but exciting and fun. In those three months, she managed to book and film a few commercials, including one large national production. Laura was on TV! Mission accomplished, right? Well, not so fast…..

As is the case with many goals, once achieved, the bar gets raised and more possibilities become apparent. It was really cool to see Laura on TV, but it was even better to witness her during filming. She absolutely loved it—all of it, make-up, wardrobe, rehearsing, and especially filming. In fact, to her, being on TV was really a side benefit. She loved to act.

So now we were presented with another moment, or perhaps just a continuation of the first. If we were going to give Laura the full opportunity to see where her acting could take her, we had to consider moving to LA permanently. Again, there were more sacrifices to consider. Financially, it was not the right thing to do. My three months away had already hurt us financially, and the cost of living in LA is definitely higher than Phoenix. Couple that with moving away from our families, who already thought we were acting irrational, and the sacrifices seemed to be much more serious. But how could we give our kid a taste of her dream, but not let her pursue it? Were we going to say something is possible and set about trying to make it happen, or rationalize that the unknown is too risky? By August of 2007, we were living in LA. In a span of nine months, we had gone from having fun with some acting classes to living in LA, me with a new job, and Danielle scaling back on her career—all for an unknown outcome. We were just enabling the dream.

Our choices came with some setbacks. The housing market in Phoenix crashed just when we decided to move, so we couldn't sell our house there for what we owed. Even with the help of family, we weren't able to keep that house and ended up losing it to the bank. To some, this created even more belief that we were acting irrationally. Enabling the dream did come at a cost. Was it worth it? If you have kids, you'll understand. Seeing your kid step out and do something you couldn't fathom doing yourself, and seeing them love it is awesome. No doubt, it was worth it. The place in Phoenix wasn't our home anymore; it was just a house. Home is where we are together, whether in happiness or struggle.

Thirteen months from the time Laura and I moved to LA to stick her toe in the water of acting for real, the big break happened. In March of 2008, just after turning eight years old, Laura found herself working alongside Adam Sandler, Keri Russell, Courtney Cox, Guy Pearce, Russell Brand, and others in Walt Disney's Bedtime Stories. It was her first feature film, and she had a lead role! Not only had her dream of being on TV been realized, but she was now going to be on the big screen. You cannot measure the pride and satisfaction Danielle and I share at seeing her take advantage of her opportunity and the sense of accomplishment in knowing we faced the moment and chose to strike out into the unknown, enabling the dream.

I suppose that could be the end of our story, but in our case, the pride and sense of accomplishment in seeing Laura on the big screen led to a second Defining Moment. We had enabled Laura's dream and helped make it come true. But what about our dreams? As I considered this, the realization set in that while the last two years had been tough, I was happy. The process of enabling Laura's dream, while completely altering our lives, brought a sense of enjoyment and purpose. I wanted to experience more of that—to create a life that enabled our family's dreams and to be more of the guy who says things are possible, then sets out to make them happen.

My job, while good by nearly anyone's standards, wasn't going to fund a lifestyle of dreams. At the same time, Danielle's playing career was coming to an end, so we were losing a significant portion of our family income. We had to step up our game and create another source of income. But how and what? Danielle and I considered a number of things, which eventually became a checklist of sorts. First, flexibility was a key consideration. If we continued supporting Laura's career, there was no way Danielle could take a typical job with a typical work schedule. We literally find out about Laura's auditions the night before, or even the day of, the audition. Whatever we did had to fit our new lifestyle in support of Laura's career. This type of flexibility also eliminated a number of business alternatives that would require a time commitment equal to a full-time job. A second consideration was finding something Danielle and I could do together. This was tougher than we realized, as there are few things that overlap between golf and electrical engineering. Third, and perhaps most important, it had to have the income potential to allow us to fund those dreams.

Our experience with Laura provided us with some insight. The residual income from her filming commercials, TV shows, and films was really an eye opener. How could we duplicate that type of income in a business model that we could build? Last, but not least, whatever we did needed to fuel our passions and allow us to do the things we really want to do. We had explored some business opportunities, but none worked out as well as we'd hoped. We knew we needed some mentorship and coaching to make it work. Through some of business opportunities and people we met, we learned about a gentleman by the name of Dean Kosage. Dean had built an incredibly successful coaching and consulting business, helping others become happy, healthy, and wealthy. Danielle and I had heard Dean speak in person on a couple of occasions, and enjoyed many more of his talks on CDs. We often spoke about our desire to be coached by someone like Dean, helping us to create the business model we desired to fund our dreams.

Call it fate, law of attraction, or perhaps divine intervention, but we came face to face with that desire. By chance, Danielle and I stopped at a café in Encinitas, CA, on our way to visit with her parents, who were vacationing nearby. Incredibly, Danielle recognized Dean Kosage walk in and sit down. Personally, I was pessimistic at the notion—the odds were against it being him. But, as fate would have it, he received a call on his cell phone, and when we heard him talking, we knew it had to be Dean. Danielle, being brave enough to speak to anyone at anytime, approached Dean to find out if it was really him. Dean was kind enough to not only spend time with us at that moment, but also invited us to meet with him later to talk in more detail about working together.

That was the second moment—although, admittedly, this was more of an opportunity than a decision. Dean presented us with an opportunity to be in mentorship with him, which we jumped at. Dean, through the new business models he is creating, is helping us to develop our passions for enabling the dreams of others, and at the same time, tying it to a new golf coaching business for Danielle. That helps Danielle continue to be involved in the game that has meant so much in her life. This is an opportunity we are still pursuing wholeheartedly, and not only do we now consider Dean a mentor, but a friend, as well. Not only is this new business allowing us to stabilize financially, we now see that it will be the vehicle to enable our dreams, as we help others with theirs.

We have come to understand when that moment comes, dare to face the unknown, be willing to take the risk, and trust that doing so for the right reasons will allow you to take advantage of the opportunities presented to you. It's amazing what you can learn from a four year old. DM

RODNEY KESLING

Over Power

ILIVED A LIFE of control, where achievement was the mark of a life well lived. This concept took root early in childhood and led me astray from the best life has to offer. However, the beauty of any given moment is that life can change. Moments of transformation open unseen doorways to places where the best of dreams give glimpses to the truth of life's abundance.

From a young age, I was responsible and took calculated actions. Raised by a single father due to the tragic car accident that claimed my mother's life, I was given the responsibility of caring for my younger sister. My demeanor was light, joyful, and kind, yet the burden of my circumstances bore heavily upon me. Even more burdensome to me was handling the sympathies of others who felt sorry for our "non-traditional" family. Sentiments rang out about "how difficult it must be to not have a mother." From the age of two, it was the only family dynamic I knew, so there was no difficulty to it.

In an attempt to repair the supposed loss that had afflicted our family, I sought to regain some status of equity insinuated by others. Conversations hung with pity: "She's a great girl, even though she has no mother." Therefore, I developed a need to fill the void others perceived by proving there was no void. My life was just as good as anyone else's life and wasn't to be measured upon a conditional scale. I sought to be free from the limitations placed on my life by the well-intended sympathies of those around me.

To accomplish this, I strove to be the epitome of excellence. I reasoned that excellence could not be understated, and I would be free from the perceived handicap of the loss of my mother. Over time, I concluded that success in all areas of my life was the way to release the grip of the widely-held stigma of pity.

I became a straight-A student and top athlete, yet with one major weakness: social interaction. By no means socially incompetent, I could socialize just fine. My confusion surrounded around how people could be so insensitive and mean. Though pity was their front, the connotation of their words crushed my desire for personal intimacy. With well-built social defenses, I interacted enough to be socially-apt, but not enough to be socially-inclined. It was a well-conceived plan to be mildly known, but avoid being the target of social inequity prompted by popularity. This, however, did not pan out. Excellence, in my mind, involved activity. Activity led to being more known, which led to popularity.

Nonetheless, I stuck with it, and achievements-over-relationships became my standard mode of operation. I planned prom, homecoming, and dozens of charity events, but failed to truly connect with others. Even, during college, amidst constant exposure and countless opportunities to do so, I continued my seemingly aloof nature. In this new stage of life, by not offering up my family situation, I felt I could avoid the stigma and subsequent pity. However, the void that pity once occupied was quickly filled with contempt. As a well-recognized, high-achieving individual, a general consensus developed that "she must think herself better than everyone else." So, I was highly-recognized, but hardly known. It didn't matter much to me then because my focus was achievement-orientated.

After college, I felt something was missing in life. Not knowing what it was, I moved to the other side of the world. My pretense was that "I didn't know the world well enough to know my place in it." I would soon discover it was me, not the world, I didn't know. Wherever I went in search for the answer, a void remained, leaving me grasping at straws. My life had become a practice of extreme grasping.

Accepting a teaching position, my travels led me to Japan. Day-in and day-out, I woke alone in my countryside home, worked in the town's schools, went home to an empty house, ate dinner accompanied by seven goldfish, and fell asleep at my desk while organizing events for charities. Throughout the year, I volunteered as a counselor and spent my summer breaks familiarizing new instructors to Japan. Needless to say, I was never wanting for something to do. Although frequently surrounded by people, I recognized the dull throb of loneliness in my life. My most intimate social interaction was with seven goldfish who presumably had no interest in how my day went.

Due to my drive for success, I was surrounded by amazing people, but did not take the time to connect with them. Life was filled with familiar smiles, brief conversations, and countless casual hugs. No substantial bonding had occurred, nor any lasting friendships built. The extent of relationships in my life was thousands of acquaintances of no particular or profound connection.

To fill the void, I decided to travel to Southeast Asia. The excitement of travel offered a getaway from the thoughts that had subversively created a deep discomfort in my heart. My plans included scuba diving lessons in Thailand, delivery of educational supplies to an orphanage in Laos, and New Years Eve in Malaysia. Little did I know, there were greater plans for me, as I embarked on my very first backpacking adventure.

I spent the first part of my trip in Thailand and came to know some of the locals who explained the Thai way of life to me. I spent my mornings learning to dive and in the afternoons, eagerly hiked to the top of a narrow staircase for a nap. My tiny attic room with a slanted ceiling wasn't tall enough to stand in, but it was the best accommodations in town for eight dollars a night. It was by no means beachfront property, but for this I would eventually be glad.

Moments of TRANSFORMATION open unseen doorways to places where the best of **dreams** give glimpses to the *truth* of life's abundance.

At night, the beach town came alive with some the most interesting spectacles I had ever witnessed. The nightlife was filled with music and lights that set the scene for a colorful clash between Thai and foreign visitors, resulting in flamboyant laughter and flirtation more appropriate for a cabaret stage than real life. On two occasions, I was fortunate to be invited to private dinners by some of the locals and gained an intimate view of Thai life. These evenings were filled with joy and loving fellowship. There were so many new experiences to witness, and I took them all in unhesitatingly with a sense of curious wonder.

It was wonderful. In under a week, I learned more about life than during all my previous years. This education was more real, more relevant, and could not be substituted by any amount of textbook learning or achievement. I had been there nearly a week and everything was better than planned. Then it happened…the moment everything changed.

It was Christmas and, unbeknownst to me, my future would be determined by my choice to either celebrate Christmas or finish my dive course. If I finished, I could finally spend a day at the beach. A week into my stay on the beautiful island and I had yet to spend time on the sun-soaked beach. Envisioned in my head, I'd go early to the beach before the crowds. However, at the last minute, I was compelled to honor the holiday and requested to finish my dive course the following day. My time on pristine beaches with gentle breezes would have to wait one more day. "The beach will still be there," I thought to myself. Although my last thought would prove ghastly in error, my choice would prove not only life changing, but also life saving.

The following day, December 26th 2004, the world experienced the largest natural catastrophe in nearly four decades. While aboard a mid-sized dive boat safely off the coast of the Thai island, we received radio notice to relinquish pursuit of our destination. That morning, tumultuous bay conditions would prove too challenging for diving. Although a picture of serenity two days prior, waves plummeted the bay, and we were advised to return to the main island. Ten minutes into our return, we were advised to stay out to sea. Radio communication relayed the impossibility of return. From the harbor shore, the ocean vanished from view, leaving a mess of sea life and anchored ships. Then… communication was cut off completely.

That afternoon, the first news we received was from a frantic relative of our fellow diver, calling from Sweden to see if he was alive and safe. The news was broadcasted around the world during our brief voyage. We left the island only two hours prior, yet the news spoke of entire islands swept over, pillaged, and inhabitants towed out to the depths of certain death. The clamor of varying reports filled the airwaves of marine VHF radios, leaving us with little understanding to what was happening. We spent the remainder of the afternoon and evening waiting to return to the island. We had no idea the sea that was our safe haven would be the same force to claim nearly two hundred thousand lives that day.

We returned to complete destruction. My heart ached, and I longed to help. There was nothing I could do. For the first time in my life, I realized my encounter with something bigger than myself. Attempting to piece together my thoughts, I was filled with disillusionment as I walked through a once lively beach town. The destruction clambered all the way to the doorstep of my guesthouse. The beautiful stretch of beach once decorated with perfectly arranged parasols and lawn chairs of varying colors was more liken to a graveyard of shipwrecked marine vessels torn into pieces. In town, sea life was found in most unbefitting places struggling for their last breaths, as unfortunate souls dragged out to sea did the same.

The following days came with stories of survivors, giving the account of those less fortunate. Heartache was the only response. Some stories spoke of those who gave their lives to save others. Some stories were about how the majority had no warning. Multiple generations of Thai families were swept to sea, annihilating entire lineages. Vacationers lost everything, many including their lives.

In these tragic moments, it occurred to me that the true importance of life was not what I had learned it to be. Standing in the departure terminal of the airport, the weight of my heart communicated the message my head struggled to understand. Posted over every inch of wall, column, door, trash bin, check-in counter, and vending machine were images of the lost. Their faces stared out from flyers and wallet-sized photos pasted to names and descriptions by those who sought to find them, hoping that just maybe someone would recognize the image and their "missing person" would still be alive. These people in search for their loved ones would not have the opportunity to physically love them ever again— find joy in their presence, embrace them in tightly-wrapped arms, or exchange a look with loving eyes. Then, it occurred to me... I had unknowingly, yet willingly, forfeited everything that meant the most in life. I neglected the one thing people hold most dear, yet it was the thing missing in my life that I desired most. That was the truth I was unwilling to confront for so long. My heart broke for these people, but, in that moment, my heart broke for me, too.

I had neglected relationships under the pretense that achievement meant or would yield more. I was missing out on the best part of life, while focused on achieving a lifestyle of success. With a broken heart, it hit me: The achievements and control were gained and maintained at a great cost. Moreover, achievements were short-lived, and I was never truly in control. Achievements are like flashes of lightening in the sky— radiant for a moment, but provide no warmth or lasting light. Relationships are like the sun—radiating with lasting light and warmth, that upon which life thrives. I paid a heavy price for meager flashes. I thought I had achieved control, yet it was an illusion I had created.

I did not have the control to save myself from the tsunami that swept over that island. I could have made other decisions on that day, and every other option would have taken my life. Whether I lived or died was not my decision, because I did not have any awareness or control of the factors. Although I perceived situations in my life were ultimately within my control, I overlooked that there is a greater power. I lived into a lie, blind by my neglect to recognize this single factor. While a painful understanding for my ego, the realization was incredibly liberating.

There were greater things at work in the world, and a greater power was in control of it all, which meant the responsibility to oversee every minute detail was no longer in my hands. It never had been. I felt like the weight of the world had been lifted. The idea of "if it's meant to be, it's up to me" vanished. In its place was the realization that I was saved for a reason. I had great purpose and was an extension of something greater than I comprehended.

After this revelation, I had a choice. I could return to my illusion of control and focus on achievement or trust in something greater and accept the opportunity to focus on things of true importance. As I processed the minutiae of this crossroad, I felt excited about the latter. The calling on my heart since childhood gave consolation that I did not need to know what waits ahead, because the promise of life is much more than I could conceive. I gave myself over to the unknown and bestowed my trust to that which had always truly been in control: God. In that moment, peace came over me, and the sun broke from the scattered clouds of my inner being. My internal storm was put to rest, and I was filled with a great promise. If I could accomplish boast-worthy achievements, then surely God could and would do more. I began to understand the constant pull on my heart toward truth— that we exist to be beacons of lights to one another and fill the earth with a radiance that will endure in the lives we touch.

I lived a life of control and achievement. Now, that controls rests with the One who can achieve far more than I could ever ask or think. Chances are He's calling you, too. I pray it doesn't take a tsunami in your life to hear Him. The joy in life is far greater than we could ever imagine and any given moment can define such understanding. Search for that moment. God can and will use all things for good to develop in each of us a light that will not be put out. DM

CRYSTAL BERG

> *The more you recognize and express gratitude for the things you have, the more things you will have to express gratitude for.*

ZIG ZIGLAR

BEHIND EVERY DEFINING MOMENT
Is A Why

SOMETIMES THE PIVOTAL MOMENT that shapes our lives escapes our recognition. Sometimes we have to be bribed to hear its message, and even then, we don't grasp its importance. As a matter of fact, for some like me, it may take years before we fully realize the impact that a person, a message, or a moment has made on our lives.

It's true – the seed to our future can be planted in front of our noses, yet we may still fail to recognize its potential to nurture our growth. I know. That seed was handed to me a long time ago—but I initially pushed it aside. Even when I did embed it into my life, I never fully appreciated the influence it had on my future or the underlying message that was being conveyed.

When I was in high school, my parents supported me and wanted me to be successful, but they knew I needed a kick start. So one day my father walked into my bedroom and handed me a book, saying "Jeremy, you've got to read this book." He sweetened the proposition with $50 cash—obviously, he knew it was going to take an incentive to motivate me to read this book, or any book for that matter. While he saw it as an opportunity to help me, I thought he was trying to change me, and I was more than a little reluctant to let him do that. But it didn't escape me that my dad had just handed me an easy way to make $50. So I merely skimmed through Zig Ziglar's, *See You at the Top*, took the money, and left the book upon my shelf, where it sat collecting dust for years to come.

Fast forward a little—I graduated from high school and moved out on my own. I landed a blue-collar job as a ski lift operator, which in turn landed me with a shoulder injury. While recovering at home with nothing else to do, the book's red cover caught my eye. It also ate at my conscience, knowing I had taken my dad's money, but I hadn't lived up to my end of the deal. Guilt got the better of me and I pulled the book from the shelf and started to right my wrongs. It was time to make an honest man of myself.

 The elevator to success is ***broken***.
If I wanted to **succeed**, I'd have to take the stairs.

By the tenth page, I was hooked. It dawned on me that my parents hadn't seen things in me that they wanted to change, but that they'd actually seen something great in me that I hadn't yet discovered. They probably knew that they could have simply told me themselves, but I wouldn't fully appreciate it. It was something I had to discover on my own, but like most young people, I needed a little nudge in the right direction. *See You at the Top* was that nudge, and its author, Zig Ziglar, was the messenger.

At the time, I knew I didn't want to be a ski lift operator for the rest of my life. I also knew that I didn't have a clue what I wanted. I wanted to be a man who went places, but had no idea where I wanted to go or how to get there. *See You at the Top* showed me that while I was searching for success and opportunity, I had no idea what that opportunity was. I also lacked the tools to get anywhere, much less where I ultimately wanted to go, which coincidently, was to the top.

I know now that I should have paid my dad for the opportunity to read that book, rather than the other way around. The lesson it taught me was profound: The elevator to success is broken. If I wanted to succeed, I'd have to take the stairs. What a concept! Until that time, I'd always looked for the easy route to success. I wanted to take the elevator all the way to the top—the stairs just seemed like too much work, a four-letter word if there ever was one.

The keys to my future success were between the covers of that book my father had to bribe me to read. In order to achieve my goals, Ziglar taught me that I had to cultivate the characteristics of success—trust, integrity, loyalty, discipline, belief, and self intent. Whew! Now I knew what I needed, but I still had to make it happen. I realized that in order to climb to the top, I needed to further my education and become a student of personal growth and development.

I never told my dad that I hadn't read Ziglar's book—and I never told him that I finally had. But I did let the words within it plant the seed that my dad had already known was there, ready to grow. The difference now was that I knew the seed was there, too. The opportunity to harvest it came on my 19th birthday when I came across a business opportunity that eventually evolved into my being named "Rookie of the Year" and an Executive Director at Excel Telecom, a company which coincidently focused heavily on personal growth.

It was in one of Excel's training seminars that I was introduced to Bob Proctor and his audio, The Success Puzzle, which taught me about the Law of Attraction. I also learned that success is defined as progressively realizing one's worthy ideal—in other words, I had to progressively move toward an idea that I loved. That's exactly what I did. By the end of the year, at the age of 22, I became Rookie of the Year in the entire country of Canada and a top income earner with an amazing team that thrived on these principles.

Today, I am the co-founder and CEO of multiple successful online companies located in Vancouver, Canada, working with people I love and respect. My companies were founded on the various principles of *See You at the Top*. While some people may identify their defining moment as their successes, I know that my successes are just stair steps on my way to the top. My true defining moment was the seed that inspired me to make the climb.

I didn't recognize my defining moment—not when it was handed to me or when I was paid to pay attention to it. Still years later, as I became a student of my own personal growth and heeded the lessons of history's best success coaches, I still failed to realize its importance. And even though I still read *See You at the Top* each and every year and have shared it with countless others along the way, I was blind to the significance of receiving the book. In my opinion, any success I'd enjoyed was the culmination of years of learning and growth, not one particular moment, person, or thing.

When I finally took the time to reflect on my past, the defining moment that had been in front of my face the whole time came to light. I needed to travel down the staircase of success to get back to where I started. The process took me back to my teenage years, back to my bedroom, and back to the very day my dad bribed me to read a book. That is when it hit me—my defining moment wasn't when I earned an award. It wasn't when I attended a fantastic seminar and learned the secrets of success. It also wasn't in any book, although there have been many which have shaped my path.

My defining "moment" actually occurred over a span of years. It began the moment my father handed me Zig Ziglar's book. The next step took place when I finally read the book. The seed was planted then, but it didn't harvest until much, much later. Just recently, after more than a decade, the "moment" which shaped my life came to completion when for the first time, I realized what my dad had been trying to tell me when he handed me a book that he thought I needed to read.

In short, I could say that receiving *See You at the Top* was my defining moment. I might choose to say that it was when I eventually got around to reading it. But I know that's not true. My defining moment came to fruition when I comprehended the importance of it, not when it occurred.

Behind every defining moment is a what and a when. What happened and when did it occur? Despite this, I found that to truly appreciate such moments, it's also necessary to comprehend the why. Sure, my dad handed me a great book, and it's also true that I (finally) read it. But it wasn't the book he shared that had the greatest impact on my life. It was the fact that he shared it because he had a belief in me, long before I believed in myself. That comprehension had escaped me for years. I now know that it was his belief that planted the seed to share the book. It was his belief that eventually fueled my desire to reach my potential. Without that belief, I'd still be on an endless elevator ride to nowhere. Instead, I'm taking the stairway to the top, one step at a time. Thank you, Mom and Dad, for seeing in me what I now see in those around me, pure potential! DM

JEREMY NICHELE

Crossroads

THERE IS AN AMAZING array of possibilities that unfold when you overcome uncomfortable situations. It is in the uncomfortable situations that you can witness your own growth and development. In life, we may encounter a "fork in the road." Many times, the path that is avoided by the ordinary allows us to be extraordinary.

Breaking Away from "Mi Familia"

I could feel my ears resonate with the sound of my own voice rebelling as my stepfather attempted to once again discipline me and prove his point. I get teary eyed, my hands start to shake, and my voice trembles with anger. My vision is blurred, yet all I could see was my mother's eyes full of martyrdom as she witnessed my stepfather slap me across the face, causing my lip to bleed. I stood in the hallway, wondering why my mother did not defend me. I heard a little girl's voice in my heart crying out for Mami, but I felt as if I was in a nightmare, yelling yet not being heard. My little sister was in her bedroom, and I could hear the trauma she experienced as she witnessed another incident. My oldest sister cried and stared at my mother in awe, wondering if Mom was going to do anything, but my mother continued to look paralyzed.

My mother stood as still as a log; she was in denial. She could not believe that her husband was mistreating her daughters. He was once a great man who provided for her daughters and raised them in a better socio-economic environment than she was able to provide on her own. My lungs filled with air as I took a deep breath and worked up the strength to swing my fist in his face and yell, "I've had enough!"

That instant was one of the biggest turning points in my life. I was 16 years old and decided to leave my household due to my stepfather's abuse and mother's incapacity to protect me. It was very difficult for me to break away from my mother and my two sisters. We were raised with strong Mexican values where "la familia" was the most important aspect of life. My mother was a single mother of three girls who were turning into three young ladies. Unfortunately, at that time, she was having difficulties in her marriage with my ex-stepfather, who resented the attention she was giving us. I realized then that living in that household had become unhealthy for me and my future.

Being a woman of Mexican-Persian heritage, I was exposed to the apparent gender differences in my cultures. Even though my father's presence in my life was really limited, the subordination of women in our culture was still apparent. Through my mother's marriages, I was able to see that a lot of the choices she made were because she did not believe she had the means to live on her own. She chose to raise a family, rather than finish her education or start a career. She sacrificed many things in order to give us what she thought was a better life. Through her experiences, I made a decision at a young age that I was going to be an independent woman and never wanted to rely on any man to give me what I wanted or needed.

In order to prepare for my break away, I did what most 16-year-olds don't want to do and got a "job." I realized that if I wanted to leave, I had to be able to financially take care of myself. I was able to start my career in financial services through a high school internship program with Washington Mutual Bank. Then, I did what most 16-year-olds want to do—I got my driver's license and bought a car. The first car I drove was a jalopy, but it got me to work and to school. I was now able to breathe my independence.

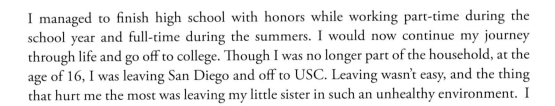

> With faith and dedication, I can *empower* my family and continue to have my own **goals** and **dreams**. That is why I decided to transition my family and *empower* them toward their own INDEPENDENCE.

I managed to finish high school with honors while working part-time during the school year and full-time during the summers. I would now continue my journey through life and go off to college. Though I was no longer part of the household, at the age of 16, I was leaving San Diego and off to USC. Leaving wasn't easy, and the thing that hurt me the most was leaving my little sister in such an unhealthy environment. I

no longer was there to protect her. However, I realized that in order to help my mother and sisters, I had to first be able take care of myself. I was struggling to take care of myself, but continued to persist through the path of independence.

I continued to work through USC, and my career continued to progress. I was one of the few students at the university who was working full-time throughout college. However, this made my education much more valuable since I was able to apply what I learned in business school to my work environment. I was blessed to be able to get financial aid and a few scholarships, so I graduated with only $33,000 in debt. With a promising career, I was now in a position where I was able to move back to San Diego and help my mother and sisters.

Back to "La Familia"

In Los Angeles, I had a life of my own and the independence I had always wanted. However, I felt lonely. Not only did I miss my family, but my family also needed me. My mother was just finalizing her divorce with my abusive ex-stepfather, and she needed guidance toward her own independence. Thankfully, I was in a position to help and was able to purchase a house for my mother and sisters the summer after I graduated from USC. Now my family could have a home. We would be a "familia" again.

I was not able to leave my career in Los Angeles until a year after I purchased the home. Yet, I was able to help sustain their household, along with my own in Los Angeles until that time. Leaving Los Angeles was very difficult for me. Los Angeles was where I was able to enjoy my freedom and accomplish my dreams—some of which I left in Los Angeles. However, San Diego had other dreams for me. It was the place where I would start the next chapter of my life and have a family—or so I thought.

Moving back gave me a sense of comfort and belonging. I no longer felt lonely and was again a part of my family. However, I still desired to have a family of my own and began to resent my family for not letting me grow. Their problems became my problems. Their struggles became my own. I started to ignore my own dreams and desires because I wanted to solve their difficulties.

This internal struggle made me realize that what brings me happiness is taking care of my family. I also realized that I don't have to give up my goals and dreams. My family never asked me to sacrifice anything for them. Like my mother, I made those choices on my own. It was truly a defining moment when I realized that I can have it all. With faith and dedication, I can empower my family and continue to have my own goals and dreams. That is why I decided to transition my family and empower them toward their own independence.

Throughout this journey of growth and independence, though, I had another relationship that affected my life and decisions. Since the age of 16, my high school sweetheart had provided me with emotional support as I strove for my independence. Unfortunately, though, because I never wanted to rely on a man to give me what I want, I never gave him a reason to do so and found myself in a relationship where I was nurturing a man who was supposed to be my partner. By doing so, I may have hindered his own personal development. Now I am facing another difficult crossroad as I decide to let him go. But I have faith—though it might not be easy, it's a choice that I must take as I reach the next crossroad in my life. And I trust that this choice, like the others I've made, is a responsible one that will ultimately take my life down the path which it was meant to follow. Until then, I'll relish the moments in my life and continue to follow my goals and my dreams, knowing that I can have it all—if I choose to do so.

Sometimes, moments present cross roads in our lives. While the decision over which direction to take can be difficult, ultimately, the choice is ours to make. I've learned to take the path that is best for me, while knowing that I don't have to give up the things or people that I hold most dear on my journey. For it is along that path that I am able to experience the extraordinary. DM

LILLIAN RAZAVI

> *The ultimate measure of a man (or woman) is not where he (she) stands in moments of comfort, but where he (she) stands at times of challenge and controversy.*

MARTIN LUTHER KING, JR.

WORK ON YOURSELF FIRST,
And The Rest Will Come

A
S A YOUNGSTER, I was diagnosed with attention deficit disorder and found it very difficult to concentrate in school, which led to seven school changes throughout my childhood. I am still uncertain whether I truly had ADD (as they called it) or if I was just another kid who had to be pushed into math, science, and geology when my personality was more aligned with english, drama, history, and anything involving human interaction. I do believe the career choices I made later in my 20's proved this theory, but we will get to that later.

Every time I travelled through the schools, I met a new network of people. Eventually, I ended up at an outdoor education program called Timbertop. I was just beginning to become involved in drinking and partying, which was the reason I was sent to this program. My family could see that if a change was not made, I could easily end up in a dark spot, something all parents fear.

After Timbertop, I went on to Geelong Grammar School, a boarding school in Victoria, and began to find my passion in photography and legal studies. Throughout my schooling, though, I continually spent my weekend breaks partying—a habit which was getting worse. This began to affect not only my reputation with teachers at school, but also my ability to stay focused was sporadic. I remember my headmaster's report card stated, "It would be nice to see Dominic come back to school from weekend breaks energized rather than exhausted and fatigued." That pretty much summed up my partying and drinking habits throughout my three high school years at GGS.

One thing which continued to stay with me since the time I was 13 years old and well into my university years was my inability to avoid drinking and drugs. This continually worsened during my studies back on the Gold Coast, which is one of Australia's premier nightclub and party cities, resulting in my increased desire to fulfil my image of a party goer with "class." The class began to slip away (if it ever existed) as more and more consumption took place. In my early 20's, I found myself developing a serious drinking problem and experimenting with ecstasy, speed, and a plethora of other drugs. During this time, I made tons of "weekend friends" and truly thought I was living the dream. That dream began to fade very quickly. I got myself into a number of risky situations while I was high. However, the addiction was in full flight, and once I got started, there was no turning back. Once, I was partying at a local nightclub and then went to an after party; however, it didn't take me long to realize that I was mingling with bikies in a place that had security cameras to keep the police out. I recall going out on Valentine's Day in 2007—as usual, I didn't have a date, so I started drinking Bacardi and Cokes, and then moved onto cocaine for the first 24 hours. Afterward, I figured I couldn't afford another day of a coke binge, so I moved on to speed. Another 24 hours later, I was back in the night clubs, drinking Vodka to try and slow my heart rate down—a move which was very logical, I thought. But like anything that stays up for so long, it must come down. This time, I was left to my own devices and cried myself to sleep, only to wake up and spend the night yelling at myself. The pain was almost unbearable. However, while it was indicative of my party days, it wasn't the worst of them.

In the end, I did finish law school and worked on the theory that if I moved back to Victoria, I could escape the partying town which was affecting me. Two months after my move, the only thing I had escaped was the shelter of my family, and it wasn't even six months before I reached what is called "rock bottom." Rock bottom is when you come to a point in your life which is at an all time low. World renowned author JK Rowling stated, "And so **rock bottom** became the solid foundation on which I rebuilt my life." This was the exact situation I was in, and, like JK, my rebuilding phase came after I encountered a moment of clarity.

During this period of my life, I was working in sales and was sent north to a state called Queensland to make a sale to a local government. During that week, I ventured home to the Gold Coast and went out drinking with some old friends. However, as usual, the "couple of drinks" ended up being an all-night session, and I woke up the next day in a mindset of self pity and angst around the issue that I couldn't seem to get out of the vicious cycle. The two months leading up to this trip had been my worst yet. I was beginning to black out and three to five hour blocks of the night would disappear. The next day, I would have to call friends to find out what I had done. Within the first 30 minutes of being at a friend's going-away party, I finished 2 bottles of white wine and was falling over people. Everyone else was on their second drink and trying to figure out what was wrong with me. As I was trying to tell a group of friends a joke, I fell backward onto a set of stairs. Wine poured all over me whilst the rest of the room laughed at me. The humiliation was painful.

I was borrowing money to live week to week and would constantly lie to my boss about being out on sales calls, when I was really in bed, unable to move because my hangovers and headaches were so intense. One morning, I wept in my living room as I came down from the previous night, thinking "will this ever end?"

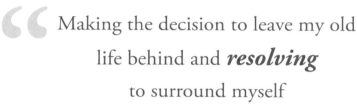

Making the decision to leave my old life behind and *resolving* to surround myself with **like-minded** people changed my life dramatically and still CONTINUES to do so.

A week before my sales trip to Queensland, I had organised to catch up over coffee with a family friend, Brad, who had once led a life of crime, drugs, and illegality; however, in a five-year period, he turned his life around and was doing amazing things around Australia, including inspiring youth to take action in their lives in a positive way. That afternoon, I caught up with Brad with the intention of telling him about my issues. However, as we sat down, he turned the meet into a one-hour reflection on my behaviour and how it required immediate attention to save my relationships and, in the end, my life. In typical 22-year-old fashion, I got quite defensive at first and put my guard up, but he pointed out that my relationship with my parents would deteriorate if I kept doing drugs, partying, and living in a self-centred state. This really hit me, and I had what some refer to as a "moment of clarity." I was truly in a state of rock bottom. I had no money, my list of friends was about as deep as the bottles of Bacardi I was throwing back, and I knew it was time to stop the humiliation. I walked away from that meeting and went straight to a local 12-step recovery meeting. When I walked in the door, people were sitting around sharing their experiences, strength, and hope. That day, the topic of the local meeting was "realization." This was quite ironic. I took immediate action from that day onward and got myself into the self-development program, which helped me get my life back on track and focus on my future.

One of the important things to address is that even though it has now been three years since this event and my life has transformed dramatically, there were some massive challenges that I had to overcome along the journey. One of the biggest changes I had to make was my environment. At that time, I had surrounded myself with people I had aspired to be like. However, once I gave away the party scene, I was rudely shocked that none of my "friends" thought I was as cool as I once was, believing my decision to give it away was insane. At 22, the peer pressure was overwhelming, and I had to make a conscious decision to break away from the people who were holding me back. I didn't make this decision on my own, but through the support and advice from my parents, Peter and Helen, whom I had formed a stronger relationship with over the years. Today, I watch a lot of people in their early 20's and late teens get caught up in some really bad environments and situations, as they are not willing to go against the status quo of their peer group. My point is your environment can either inspire you or expire you. Making the decision to leave my old life behind and resolving to surround myself with like-minded people changed my life dramatically and still continues to do so.

Another challenge I had to overcome was in the way I saw myself. After years of hanging out with the wrong crowd and indulging in behaviour which decimated my self-image, I had a lot of personal development to do to change the opinion I had of myself and what I could accomplish. Watching the success my parents had in their business and personal life, I thought they would be a great couple to model to help elevate my life to another level. Personal development through reading and learning new concepts was something new to me, though, and at first I found it very confronting. However, I took the approach that I had nothing to lose and everything to gain by immersing myself. One of my life heroes, Dexter Yager, stated, "Success begins by raising the opinion we have of ourselves." I couldn't agree more.

Along the journey of personal development, one of my mentors introduced me to a strength and conditioning program called CrossFit. At the time, I was finding great mental and physical balance through exercise and had essentially taken it up as a new passion. CrossFit can be described as the exercise program Navy Seals, police, MMA fighters and soccer moms use to get functionally fit. It's high intensity and tests you both mentally and physically on a daily basis, which I have come to relish. One of the biggest things I have learned is the importance of discipline. Both in my business and personal life, I have found the greatest success comes from discipline toward a goal. The discipline I put into diet and my exercise helped me lose 40 pounds in 9 months and has helped me keep it off.

Through all of these activities, as well as creating a new friendship circle, I have managed to not only raise the opinion I have of myself, but have taken it to a level I never thought possible. Overcoming the challenges brought on by my drinking and drug issues has allowed me three years of a life I never thought possible. I eventually found a job in the legal world and began working in a small law firm; however, I found that after three years at university and a year into the industry, being a lawyer was not for me and my real passion was in dealing with people.

Around that time, I took on a role with an energy drink company that had come to Australia a few years prior and have since helped that company grow another 2 million in sales, which has been a great achievement for all of us. Through working with that company and since forming my own business, I have been able to find my passion in dealing with and empowering people to take action in their lives.

One of the biggest gifts I have been given in this short journey is the relationship I have formed with my fiancée, Karina. I never thought during my drinking and drugging that I would find true love; however, time has shown me that anything is possible. With my family, I managed to help create a large youth program, which is held annually in Australia and has seen over 700 youth between 16 and 26 years of age come through our 7-day "camp," which focuses on leadership, teamwork, self-development, and being outdoors. This has been, and will continue to be, a big part of my life. Through this program, I learned the philosophy that "you can have anything you want in life, if you can help enough people get what they want," a quote taken from the great Zig Ziglar. DM

DOMINIC McKENNA

"I am here for a ***purpose*** and that purpose is to grow into a mountain and not shrink into a grain of sand."

OG MANDINO

Tribulations and Blessings

GROWING UP IN a middle-class family in Queens, New York, and later on moving to New Jersey in the early 80s, I was the only son born to my parents, Razia and Kausar Zaidi. Being the youngest child, I had two older sisters, and my life was normal until the fourth grade. In the fifth grade, though, that all changed. As the only son in the family, I unexpectedly had to step up into the role of man of the household, a position which ultimately changed the man I became and my entire life.

I remember, like it was yesterday, the day my father had his first heart attack, just as well as I remember the subsequent health problems that my dad faced. That first heart attack launched others, and my dad not only suffered cardiovascular problems and a stroke, but he was also diagnosed with diabetes. Caring for him became my mom's full-time job—even though she already had a full-time job in a retail store to support our family.

My father was a role model who earned my respect, as well as the respect and love of everyone who knew him. Not overly religious or wealthy, he was rich in character and personality, thinking nothing of helping someone in need, even when he had little to give. He was the kind of man who would take the shirt off his own back and hand it to someone else with a smile.

My mom was a super woman in my eyes and within our community and family. She never complained about financial difficulties, or a lack of dining, shopping, or socializing. She simply devoted every moment of her time to her husband and children. My mother awed people with her amazing cooking skills and somehow managed to make our home look like a million bucks on a very limited income. She took charge of my dad's health, watching his diet and making sure he got to his doctor appointments and took all his 20 different medications throughout the day. She perfected the roles of wife and mother with love and care, balancing each in such a way that it seemed natural and effortless, regardless of the obstacles that came her way.

My dad was sick for 15 years, but during that time, I was blessed to be able to see the pride in his face when I graduated from Rutgers University with a Major in Public Health and Medicine. I remember visiting him in the hospital, where he had spent so much of his time, the day before he passed away. Call it a gut feeling, if you will, but somehow I knew that February 24th, 2008 would be the last day I would see my father alive.

Dad's death shook our entire family, especially my mom, who had devoted her life to caring for him. His loss left a huge void in her life, leaving her feeling empty and unneeded. It became my job to take her to the cemetery several times a week, and I'd watch, heartbroken, as she would cry and pray for him at his grave.

In the summer of 2009, my uncle's family arrived from Dubai, bringing with them their condolences and a sincere attempt to boost our family's morale and energy levels. Their visit injected some cheer back into our home, and Mom enjoyed having family around. We even held a surprise party to celebrate her 52nd birthday on August 7,

2009. My uncle joined his family about a month later, and my mom was excited to see him. The night of his arrival, she was smiling as she said goodnight to everyone. It seemed normalcy was returning to our home. On August 14th at 4 a.m. the next morning, though, she wandered through the house, talking very loudly before walking into my room, looking confused and helpless. She was unconscious by the time the ambulance got her to the hospital. Centra State Hospital diagnosed her with a brain-related illness; she was then transferred to Overlook Hospital, where the doctor's found a malignant brain tumor known as Multiform Glioblastoma at Stage 4. They gave my mom a few months to a year to live.

During my entire childhood, it was my mom who was the strong, healthy one in our family, or so called "The Rock." Dad had always been sick, but now just months after his death, my mom was fighting for her own life; the sad part was that she didn't even know it. And her illness was even more debilitating than my dad's. The craniotomy surgery, which was an attempt to remove multiple tumors in her brain, left the right side of her body paralyzed. Her speech was severely impaired, and when she did talk, it was usually to ask about my dad. Obviously, the tumors had affected her memory and she couldn't remember that he was gone from this world.

I chose to remain in denial. At the time, I couldn't deal with the loss of another parent. I became extremely angry at anyone and everyone—I hated the world. And I lost my faith. I couldn't talk to anyone—my feelings were too difficult, and yes, too painful, to describe. After all, my mom had been my saving grace when I lost my dad—how could I possibly lose her, too? So I didn't express my emotions; I just continued working full-time, spending my days at Ricoh as a Medical Sales Executive, and then

"Live amongst people in such a manner
that if you die, they weep over you

and if you are alive,
they crave for your company."

IMAM ALI

visiting my mom as often as I could every day.

Mom's illness took a toll on her, and on me, as well. Her treatments required seven hospital changes as her illness quickly progressed. Eventually, my mom's deteriorating health spurred me to resign from my job at Ricoh—she was the only thing that mattered to me at that time. Spending every possible moment comforting her, I watched her endlessly, like she watched me when I was an infant. During the last month of her life, I wouldn't leave the hospital and stayed overnight, every night, as her condition became increasingly critical.

The day she passed, I was with her until 2 a.m. before I left to go home to get some fresh clothes and catch a few hours of sleep. The next morning, my sister, Shiggo, called to tell me that Mom was in bad shape and I should come right away. I drove about 90 mph to get to the nursing home and ran to my mom's room. My sister held me back from going into the room and told me that Mom was no longer with us. In shock, I went into her room and held her hand, frozen and unable to do anything else. Yes, I was in shock—although I knew in my heart that she was very sick and her illness was severe, I had hoped that God would step in and she would get better. All I wanted to know was why God chose for me not to be present when she took her last few breaths...why? I will never know.

Being the only man left in the family, I held myself together for the sake of my sisters and to make the funeral arrangements. It was my responsibility and strongest desire to make sure my mom's funeral was done properly and with the utmost honor and respect for her life and character.

My mom's passing awakened my spirituality. As a Shia Muslim, we believe in one god, the prophet, the Quran and Ahulbayt. The Ahulbayt is basically the prophet's household—we consider them to be divine and the mentors who had set an example for us to follow on this earth. The grandson of the prophet had lost his entire family while standing up for justice in Karbala, Iraq. This and other trials and tribulations experienced by the Ahulbayt made my circumstances seem minuscule. With that realization, I was drawn toward a spiritual journey, what is known as a pilgrimage, and decided to go to Iraq and Syria. The purpose of this trip was twofold—to complete my mom's last wish and to transform my thought process in an attempt to realize what is important in this life.

My mom had been a very pious and spiritual Muslim woman who faithfully performed all of her religious duties. One of her last wishes had been to go on a journey called Ziyarat. While I wanted to carry out my mom's last wish and gain an understanding of the importance of earthly life, I also knew that I needed an escape from the empty, lonely environment I had left behind. (*This was the first time I had traveled outside of the United States since I was a child, and I went with no expectations*).

My journey took me to Iraq and Syria, where I spent time in cities like Najaf, Kufa, Karbala, and Damascus. I have to admit that it was both humbling and rewarding. When I visited my first shrine in Syria, I could feel my mom's presence with me, and it gave me peace in my heart that I was doing the right thing for her.

I spent the majority of my time in deep prayer and meditation. The trip gave me a special appreciation for the Iraqi people. It was surely a blessing to meet them. The void in my life began to be filled with spirituality, peace, and a newfound understanding of my existence. As a result, I learned to accept the reality of death, as well as the meaning of life. In the end, I realized that all that matters is the kind of person you are, regardless of how much time you're given on Earth, it's all about the deeds you carry out.

However, when I returned to New Jersey, I had to endure another setback and disappointment as I went through the loss of our family home. More than a house, it was a sentimental attachment to my parents, and a symbol of the shelter and security they had provided me throughout my life. It was also the holder of the memories of all that was gone. Every inch of the house represented my mom's sense of décor and my dad's hard work.

I had no control over the State's actions *since death does not come to us as planned.* Unfortunately, I had to forfeit our home due to my mother's unpaid medical expenses by Medicaid. With no parents, no home, and no job, I decided to move to Houston, where my eldest sister, Diba, resides. I got back on my feet and found work as a Technology Sales Executive. About a month later, however, I encountered yet another challenge. This time, the health problems I faced were my own. I had major kidney problems that had developed a severe infection, causing scar tissue and extreme complications. I couldn't eat or drink anything and was kept on IV antibiotics. As a result, I had to resign my new job, leaving me again with no income or health insurance. For four months, I was bedridden in between hospitalizations and three different surgeries. The pain, which was pure agony, was compounded by the loss of my house, my job, and most of all, my parents.

After losing everything, the only thing that I had left was my health—now it, too, was failing me. The emotional and physical healing from losing all the necessities of my life took a long time, but as my health improved, so did my outlook. It became a time of curiosity and retrospect. I wondered why God had made me go through so much. I reflected on the events in my life and realized that He had a purpose. Maybe becoming ill afforded me an opportunity to heal emotionally from everything else that had happened—something which I had not fully allowed myself to do.

My *experiences* made me the **man**
I am today
and created within me the
FUEL and ENERGY to take control
and make my *mark* in **life**.

Maybe it was God's way of making sure that I appreciated what I did have—my health. Once I got my health back, I was so thankful and blessed for the many things I had taken for granted. I could eat, walk on my own, and was mobile again. This was God's way of saying, *"If you think you have it bad, think again, it can always get a lot worse." This perception embarked in me a fuel of positive energy and optimism.*

Having this perception led me to a new outlook on life and as a person. This was my defining moment. My experiences made me the man I am today and created within me the fuel and energy to take control and make my mark in life.

The man I am today is based on my life experiences and the way my parents raised me. Because my dad had been so sick for so long, I had to grow up fast. After losing my parents, I learned that nothing matters in life except the deeds and actions that reveal my true, genuine character. I know now that one should strive for the worthiness of a mother and father and family. We should not take family for granted because we never know when they might leave us. Because of my parents' examples, I surround myself with good-hearted people that bring out the best in me. The world is full of good people—and by finding and surrounding myself with them, I am a better person.

I've also learned that life is too short not to enjoy the things you love. Today, I take time for the things that I'm passionate about—playing soccer, spending time with family and friends, and remembering my loved ones. I choose to expand myself in every way I can to become a better person—to take control of my health, my finances, my career, my relationships, and my spirituality. I have so much to do and so much to be thankful for, but in order to come to that realization, it was necessary for me to overcome the tribulations that came my way. It was a wise man, indeed, who said that God gives hardships to people in the amount they can only handle and bear.

I've learned that those misfortunes served as stepping stones which guided me toward a greater understanding of my purpose and an appreciation for the many blessings I've been given, for it is those trials and tribulations that have defined me and made me the better person I am today. DM

ALI ZAIDI

"A person often meets his *destiny*
on the road he took to avoid it."

JEAN DE LA FONTAINE

TRUST AND LISTEN TO
Your Little Voice

WHILE HAVING A FUN girls' night out with my sister, Marcia, I was sitting on a stool in a restaurant lounge in Orange County and listening to her favorite band when my attention was jolted by a man and women entering the lounge. Immediately, I heard my little voice say, "You need to meet that man." Now, I did not know if they were married, and I didn't feel a physical attraction, but the message was very strong and clear…you need to meet this man. They were both in their thirties, well dressed, and could have been husband and wife—I didn't really know, but I knew I needed to meet him.

My life at the time, though outwardly successful, was in inner turmoil. I wanted more in life. I was a big thinker even back then, but didn't know how to get what I wanted. My career path was headed in a good direction—as Director of Marketing for a high-end placement agency in California, I had been in my industry for 10 years and thought a corporate presidency was in my future. The reality was I was drinking too much, doing social drugs, and I was frustrated and angry.

So there I sat on the stool watching the couple, wondering if I should or shouldn't go up and talk to them. I didn't want it to seem to the woman as though I was hitting on her husband or date. I sat, and I sat, and I sat…should I, shouldn't I? Several times I thought, *oh forget it, this is stupid, I'm not going to make a fool of myself.* Then I thought, but what *if I DO really need to meet him and I don't do anything and they leave?* The question I asked myself was, "Do I have the courage to make a fool of myself?"

All of a sudden, she stood up… I thought, oh, could they be leaving? Not sure, oh, she was going to the ladies room. I immediately jotted down my name and phone number and rushed over to his table, as though I really was stealing her man. I blurted out, "Hi, my name is Denice, and I know this is going to sound weird, but I had a little voice tell me when you walked in that I needed to meet you, I don't know why but here's my number, please call me. Oh, this isn't a come on, I just think we need to meet." And away I went. My fear of missing out on something important was greater than the fear of making a fool of myself; 20 seconds of courage changed many lives.

We finished our evening, and I kept feeling, I NEED TO KNOW THIS MAN.

There are moments in our lives that occur and we don't even know that "life as we know it will never be the same." This was one of those moments.

Sitting in my office a few days later, I received a call. The gentleman said, "My name is Mike Weinberger; I met you at the restaurant the other night." My heart skipped a beat.

He asked, "What can I do for you?" At that point, I really don't remember what I said other than, "I was just sitting there and when you walked in with your wife, (assuming she was his wife), I heard a little voice say, 'you need to meet that man.'"

I asked, "What do you do?" Well, when he explained that he was working for a man named Jim Rohn and they did seminars teaching people how to live life by design rather than a life by default, I was hooked. It was exactly what I needed to hear at that time in my life.

We often do not trust that our little voice is there to serve us. I truly believe it is a little nudge God is giving us. If you hear and heed the voice, you will learn to trust it. You may never know what could have or would have happened if you do not listen to your little voice, but I for one am certainly glad that I had the courage to listen to my little voice that night, not really knowing that LIFE AS I KNEW IT WOULD NEVER BE THE SAME. Since then, life has been a wild ride. What I wanted was a life filled with passion, love, travel, and the ability to touch and affect lives in a positive way, and, boy, that's exactly what I've gotten.

As I have shared with many audiences over the years, sometimes that little voice can save your life, enhance your life, or change your life, but if you don't listen to it, you will never know. That little voice can be saying nothing more than *you should bring a jacket today,* or *don't lock the door today,* or *don't put the baby there, or you should talk to that person.* Women may call it their sixth sense or intuition, but it happens to men, as well. It's that little voice that is so easy to ignore, and sometimes overlooked, but in the cases where we heed the advice, it can change our lives.

The decision to listen to that little voice that day not only changed my life, my parents' lives, and my entire family's lives, but thousands of others lives, as well. Let me explain. Jim Rohn, who you may have heard about, was a simple man with profound insight and wisdom. Jim spoke all over the world to audiences about personal development. He taught us how to live life on our terms, how to care for one another, and be a better version of ourselves. He was a master communicator and mentor to many of the change agents around the world, people like Anthony Robbins and many, many other thought leaders. Just about every self-help and personal development speaker today learned from or knows Jim's material. Well, Mike Weinberger introduced me to the world of Jim Rohn, and as I said, I was hooked. I loved his message, I loved his depth, and I loved his delivery.

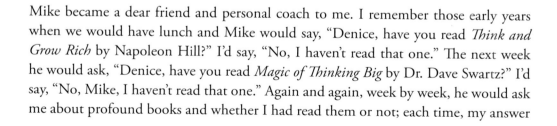

I had the courage to listen to my **little voice** that night, not really knowing that LIFE as I knew it would *never* be the same.

Mike became a dear friend and personal coach to me. I remember those early years when we would have lunch and Mike would say, "Denice, have you read *Think and Grow Rich* by Napoleon Hill?" I'd say, "No, I haven't read that one." The next week he would ask, "Denice, have you read *Magic of Thinking Big* by Dr. Dave Swartz?" I'd say, "No, Mike, I haven't read that one." Again and again, week by week, he would ask me about profound books and whether I had read them or not; each time, my answer was always the same. "NO, I HAVEN'T READ THAT ONE." Finally, one day I told him, "Mike, don't you get the message that I don't read? I did in school and think I'm pretty smart, I don't want to read anymore." His response was profound…"Well, Denice, don't you get it? You should read." Wow, did that change my life.

Adventures in Reading was a program that Jim Rohn Productions was marketing, and Mike was a regional manager. I bought a ticket to the class, and it changed my life. WOW, a whole new world opened up to me and gave me insights I had no idea existed, like how to actually read a book without falling asleep in the first 10 minutes—what a concept. This program started me on a lifelong habit and enjoyment of reading. Mike asked me if I would be open to marketing Jim's seminars, and I believed so much in the programs I decided to start marketing them.

There are times in everyone's life when opportunity knocks. We will embrace the opportunity, reject the opportunity, or research it long enough that it simply disappears. I made the decision to embrace the opportunity, and I quit my job and started marketing personal development seminars. Attending all the seminars with Jim's company allowed me to be introduced to new thoughts, new ideas, and new concepts and allowed me to understand that we are all in control of our lives—if it is to be, it's up to me. Leaving the corporate world to become an entrepreneur was the beginning of a whole new life.

Shortly after meeting Jim Rohn, I begged my father to come to one of his speeches. At the time, my father was in his 50's, angry, frustrated and drinking too much. He was a prominent corporate executive for a fortune 500 company. He was always very involved in the community, had been school board president, homeowners president, founder of our local YMCA, and community leader. My father wasn't home very often, but when he was home, he was not very happy. I've learned since then that he was a winner in a losing situation. The corporate world had sucked out every bit of my father's positive spirit; he was drowning in his unhappiness. It became more and more apparent to me that my negative father just might be helped by Jim's teaching. Again, I was listening to that little voice. I begged him, saying, "If you never do anything for me the rest of my life, please come hear Jim speak." His comment was, "I don't need all that positive crap." My mom, my best friend and mentor, was a successful bank executive. In her wisdom, she convinced him to support my new career path by saying, "Honey, this is obviously important to her, we should support her." So they came. Again, it became a moment when life as we knew it would never be the same. Mom and Dad came to a few events, and their life was changed, like mine.

Listening to that little voice was the beginning of what would be a life path, creating a legacy for our family and many others. A short three months later, my father, who was a corporate executive, was introduced to network marketing. To this day, Dad says if he had not been introduced to Jim Rohn's teaching prior to hearing about network marketing industry, he would never have been open minded enough to really see the opportunity presented him.

In order to live a life of passion and purpose, we need to take some risks and learn to trust ourselves. As you develop your little voice listening skills, you will notice that sometimes that little voice sends you into uncomfortable situations, sometimes even giving you ideas that go against your own logic! Taking action usually doesn't cause regret; however, not taking action many times does result in a "WHAT IF" life.

There are thousands of examples of people having courage to listen to their little voices; the courage is to trust your little voice, trust it will serve you. Have the courage to do what your little voice is telling you. As long as it doesn't harm anyone, listen…take your jacket, take that job, don't go in that direction, or don't take that plane, maybe even don't marry that person.

Life can get crazy busy—going, doing, being, and seeing all the things in life that are going on around us can be deafening. Sometimes we just need to slow down, quiet our mind and listen. Don't just LIVE your life—take a moment to be IN your life. Rushing around sometimes cause us to miss an important message. Think back on a moment when you listened to your little voice and the outcome was amazing. Then think about a time when you didn't listen—what was the outcome? I have found over the years that when I listened, it was much more productive than when I didn't.

As I speak to audiences, I challenge them to TRUST their little voice. The message I leave them with is that most times when we are at a crossroads in life, WE KNOW WHAT TO DO, if we listen to that little voice. To young women, I ask, if you are out for the evening with a young man and the thought crosses your mind…*I shouldn't go with him*, or *I shouldn't trust him*, or *I don't think this is a good idea*…LISTEN TO YOUR LITTLE VOICE. I'm not saying you should make your decisions out of fear, I'm just saying listen to your inner voice. If you are interviewing for a job and the thought crosses your mind…*I need to take this opportunity if they offer it to me,* chances are you may be right. Make sure the voice is coming from your inner being, not your fears, or even your hopes, but your real inner soul. An exercise I use in workshops when people are trying to learn to listen to their little voice is to have them ask themselves,

"What do I think I need to do?" Okay, take a deep breath and ask yourself again, "What do I need to do?" Then take a deeper breath and ask yourself again, "What do I know I need to do?" By asking three times and really taking time to listen each time, you will learn to listen to that little voice, and it will serve you well. Most of us hear that little voice daily, and sometimes it really doesn't make a tremendous impact on our lives, but if we get into the habit of NOT listening to that little voice, we might dismiss it at a very crucial time in our life.

If I had only one lesson to leave to my children, family, friends, and the next generation, it would be: have the courage to trust and listen to your little voice; it will serve you well. In some cases, it can save your life and can lead you to an amazing life. DM

DENICE MORALES KENNEDY

Learn to **trust** and listen to your little VOICE.

What is it telling you *now?*

DENICE MORALES KENNEDY

Destiny

THOSE FORTUNATE ENOUGH to recognize life's defining moments become the benefactors of their rewards. The moment which shaped my life came at such a young age that I almost didn't grasp its message. In fact, I did everything I could to push it aside and take a different path.

Fourteen years old and about to enter high school, I grew up in a very poor family. However, school and sports promised to offer me an abundance of opportunities. Academically, I was an overachiever. My grades were stellar, and the potential for scholarships was more of a certainty than a possibility. My athletic abilities invited even more interest from schools that were eager to include me on their rosters. I was named number one in the Capital Area Wrestling League and an All-Star in the MD/VA League. Elite high schools like Bullis in Potomac, Maryland, and DeMatha in Hyattsville had offered me full scholarships based on my grades and wrestling achievements. So as you can see, I was young, but I had the world at my feet. It wasn't a lack of opportunities that stood in my way—my only problem was that I had too many choices, if that's possible.

Adding to those choices was my mom's deep desire for me to attend an Islamic school.

Her wish went against everything that I so very much yearned for in my life. It was an option that offered no future for a scholar and athlete. In fact, Islamic school paled in comparison to private schools, which had it all—this was my one chance to live the American Dream and become a successfully Ivy League academic star and jock! Private schools were my entryway to the college of my choice and unlimited potential in anything I wanted to do for the rest of my life. If only I could make my mom understand everything I would be giving up to follow her dream instead of mine.

The only problem was that at the same time I was faced with these choices, I was slowly losing my sense of self.

The summer before ninth grade was one I'll never forget. Who doesn't remember their first drink of alcohol? As a matter of fact, it was a summer spent without caution, full of lots of fun and lots of trouble. With careless spontaneity, I partied hard, getting both drunk and high for the first time in the same few weeks. Sure, I knew the risks of such behavior and the possibility that it could negatively impact my future academic and wrestling careers, but I didn't take that possibility seriously. I'd gotten away with things in the past and still excelled, so I reasoned that this wasn't any different. I justified my behavior by telling myself that I could handle it—no problem.

Growing up in an Islamic household and being a Muslim, though, such activities were strictly forbidden. I knew that and did my best to hide my partying from my parents… and I even thought I'd actually gotten away with it. Then one day in the middle of the summer, out of the blue, my mom offered to send me to camp. But it wasn't a camp where kids go to hike, sit around a campfire, and sleep under the stars—no, this was a camp where I could connect to and strengthen my spirituality. The first thing that

entered my mind was "Why? Why me? Why now? Had she found out what I'd been up to?" Maybe not...maybe she just thought I was bored. Regardless of her motive, I didn't want to go. I was having too much fun to leave for a week of spirituality camp.

> Sometimes, though, we don't have total control over our **destinies** and something *intercedes* to map our course in a much DIFFERENT WAY than we envision.

Sometimes, though, we don't have total control over our destinies and something intercedes to map our course in a much different way than we envision. That's what happened to me. Adamant that I did not want to attend a spirituality camp, I didn't think there was anything that would change my mind. Then one night while lying in bed, something came over me—an invisible and unthinkable change of heart—and suddenly I knew that not only was I going to go this camp, but I also wanted to go. Although I didn't recognize it at the time, this became one of my defining moments.

The week I spent at camp was totally awesome! It wasn't a lot of spiritual activities that made it so great, but rather it was the camaraderie and power of associating with peers and role models who made a profound impact on me. While I had spent the majority of my summer doing the wrong things, they positively influenced me to do the right thing. In a week's time, I regained my footing and was on solid ground. I got back in touch with my upbringing and reconnected with my spirituality.

On the last day of the camp, we performed a spiritual exercise that required us to stay up from dawn until sunrise the next morning, spending the entire time meditating and praying. Believe me, there was a lot of time for reflection. It was during this exercise that I was truly awakened and could see that God was laying my choices in front of me. I could choose whatever path I wanted, veering to the right or the left. Did I want to live my life as I had during the first half of the summer, or continue on this new spiritual path on which I'd just embarked? What about sports? Scholarships? College? Money? Fame? Girls? Are those the things that I wanted in life, and did I want them enough to risk my spirituality? On the other hand, I could go to an Islamic school which offered no sports, poor academics, and very little chance of advancement and networking; however, my spirituality could remain intact. My choices were many, but they were at such complete opposite ends of the spectrum.

I was only 14 years old and at a major crossroad in my life. Whichever path I chose would ultimately determine my entire future. If ever there was a defining moment, this was it. I had to make a decision that I could be at peace with for the rest of my life—hopefully, one I'd never regret. With a great deal of soul searching and prayer, I knew by the time I got home which path I would pursue. I decided to give up my Ivy League dreams and a pursuit of the worldly life for the sake of learning about who I am and mainlining my faith.

It was with that defining moment that my journey to discover my true self commenced.

I went on to Islamic school, just as my mother intended. However, I definitely did not fit in among the other students. I was used to larger schools and larger classes. My class consisted of only eight students, four guys and four girls. In addition, the level of teaching was far below what I was accustomed to—instead of being in high school, it felt like I was back in junior high. You could say that I was ahead of the class. Also, I was way too "out there" for most of my classmates, with their conservative clothing and meek personalities. But even though they didn't all have a crazy and wild personality and past like me, I sensed something special about them—they had an internal peace and understanding that I respected and longed for in my own life. So while it appeared that we all wanted the same thing, it was their manners and politeness that I didn't yet possess.

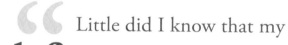

" Little did I know that my **defining moment** would change my life FOREVER and lead me to a path where worldly possessions and faith are both *possible*. "

My new classmates also spoke multiple languages, an area which did put them ahead of me academically. Learning and mastering those languages was one of the many benefits I received from choosing the path less traveled. It was also through this path and this choice that I realized that I didn't have to sacrifice one thing for another. I didn't have to choose between my spirituality and a successful career, like I had previously thought. I could excel academically and spirituality and enjoy the best that both worlds have to offer. Little did I know that my defining moment would change my life forever and lead me to a path where worldly possessions and faith are both possible.

Today, I am world traveler, and I fluently speak three languages. I own and run a successful global company and have made connections from all over the world, including Sharon Lechter and Dean Kosage, both incredible individuals whom I admire very much. They are champions at what they do, and their achievements are plentiful. Each of these connections is a part of my life's ultimate plan.

I've learned to recognize my defining moments and know it is precisely those moments that have shaped my destiny. My defining moments have led me to a life that is more enriching and full than I ever imagined or could have obtained in any other way. What does the future hold? I'm not certain, but I do know that the defining moments of my youth have already impacted my life and provided me with happiness and success, as well as an inner peace that can only come from being true to myself and the spirituality that has shaped me. I admit that it's not the future I envisioned when I was 14 years old and dreamed of being a member of the Ivy League and sports fame. It's better.

Recognize your defining moments. Trust them and follow them to your destiny. I'm glad I did. DM

HUSEIN MALIK

THE MOTHER I NEVER
Thought I Could Be

A S CHILDREN, most of us dream of being something "spectacular," such as an actress, an astronaut, a doctor, a firefighter, and many other titles our parents inspire us to be. That wasn't my dream. As a young girl, I was always unsure what I wanted to be when I grew up. No matter how hard I thought about it, nothing ever came to mind. I drew a blank. As a student, I always managed to get good grades and was not really interested in sports. Like most teenagers, I just went with the flow and made sure I would graduate. When I finally got that seemingly pointless diploma in 1997, I found myself going to a nearby community college. I was forcing myself to go through what felt like an extension of high school, simply because I was trying to please my parents. After only a semester and a half, I couldn't do it anymore. College wasn't what I wanted, so it was time to walk away. Still unsure what to do with my life, I decided to enter the work force. My first job was at a physical fitness center in the daycare department. It wasn't glamorous by any means, but it was money in my pocket. From there, I moved on to a receptionist job at a car dealership. It was easy for the most part, but again, nothing that I wanted to endure for the next 20 years. So I decided I would answer phones by day, and at night, I would attend a nine-month program to become a Medical Assistant.

At this point, I was trying to find a way to make money without having to go to school again for another 4 to 7 years. So I chose the medical field. After nine months of anatomy, fancy medical terms, and being poked at with needles, I graduated. It wasn't a fancy PHD, but it was an accomplishment for me, nonetheless. I did it—by myself and for myself. My first medical assistant job was at a pediatric office. I skipped around doing odd jobs throughout the day, but I never found myself doing many of the medical assistant duties my $9,000 certificate had trained me to do. However, I was getting paid more than I would if I worked in the back office. So, I stayed in the front office. Again, I found myself doing what I had to do to get a paycheck. Don't get me wrong—I was very blessed with the opportunities I was given, and I loved everyone that I worked for, but I still wasn't happy. Why would I be? I wasn't doing anything I enjoyed. Unfortunately, too many people live that way. I wasn't going to be one of them.

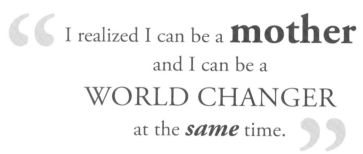

I realized I can be a **mother** and I can be a WORLD CHANGER at the *same* time.

During my seven-year sentence in the medical office, I became engaged to the man who stole my heart back when I was a senior in high school. We had managed to stay together, even through his crazy lifestyle as a traveling pro baseball player. It wasn't easy by any stretch of the imagination. From the time he started college, my life revolved around him. I don't mean that in a bad way—it's just the way it was. I would travel all over to watch him play. He was living his dream, and I wasn't going to let him live it without me. Besides, there was nothing exciting going on in my life. I was working six days a week to provide for us and pay the bills. That was my life. I figured at least one of us was living out their childhood dream.

At this point in my life, I started to realize what my true passion was. I had already found the love of my life—there was only one part missing. I wanted a family. Having grown up in a very family-oriented home, a family was and still is one of the most important things to me. I found myself saying that all I wanted to do was be a mother. I knew it in my heart, and it was what I had been trying to figure out my whole life up until that point. So, we got married in 2003, and after two more years of working the grind, I was able to quit my job. My husband had retired from baseball due to a career-ending injury and was making enough money in his traditional business in the mortgage industry to allow me to stay home. Before too long, I was pregnant, and in December of 2007, I gave birth to a bouncing baby girl.

At that defining moment in my life, I knew I had the dream job I had always wanted. How is it possible to only know someone for a few seconds and love someone so much? I was in love for the second time in my life, and all I wanted to do was be a good mother. From the moment I brought her home, I did everything I thought I needed to do to fill that title as the world's best mom. I was definitely not perfect, but I was doing my best. I soon found myself having many hats of those fancy careers everyone talked about. In no time, I became a teacher, a nurse, a counselor, a cook, a housekeeper, a referee, and other roles I probably don't even realize. I decided I wasn't going to be all of these things to her and my future children until the age of 18, like television portrays parenthood. I was going to be there for her for anything she needed until the day I die. For this reason, I believe that being a parent is the most difficult job anyone can ever have, but at the same time, the most rewarding. But while I juggled my many roles, I realized something that I was not—I was no longer myself. I was trying so hard to be the perfect mother and wife that I stopped doing things for myself. I stopped taking care of myself, not just physically, but mentally. I always put myself last. If there was time left at the end of the day and I wasn't too tired, I could do something I actually enjoyed. For the most part, though, I was just too tired.

Recent events in my life have given me the opportunity to grow in a way I never knew I could. I realized I can be a mother and I can be a world changer at the same time. You see, I have discovered that there is so much more to being a good mother than what I had been doing. I learned that I also need to be an example to my children. I need to be an example of what is to be ambitious, a go-getter, a dreamer, a visionary. It wasn't until my eyes were opened to possessing these characteristics that I knew I wanted to have that example in myself. My husband has always had these types of qualities. To him, they came naturally. I guess I have always had them, too. I was born that way. God has always intended for me to persevere and live in abundance; He was just patiently waiting for me to find it within myself. Eureka!

So, here I am today, sharing with you a series of events that have led to the self-discovery of my true capabilities. The only thing I ever wanted to be had so much more potential than what I was living it out to be. I was being stretched. The quiet girl that I had always been was now doing things like leading a team, speaking on stage, and now, being a co-author in a book. For whatever reason, I had previously tattooed in my brain that there was a very narrow definition of being a good mother. Little did I know there was so much more, and I had the potential to be more. I am now not only living life for my daughter, I am living it for myself. And in doing so, I am showing my child that life isn't about having to choose only one path. I am an example, too, that you can accomplish as much as you desire. As long as you have drive and determination, you can do anything. Perhaps having a child was the reason my eyes were opened to my true God-given abilities. Maybe I would have discovered them in another way. But either way, I am now living out my dream—my dream to change people's lives, change the world, but most importantly, to do it while being an example to my daughter, showing her what it means to never give up on anything, including herself. DM

ROCHELLE PATTERSON

> *God has always intended for me to*
> *persevere and live in abundance;*
>
> *He was just patiently waiting*
> *for me to find it within myself.*

ROCHELLE PATTERSON

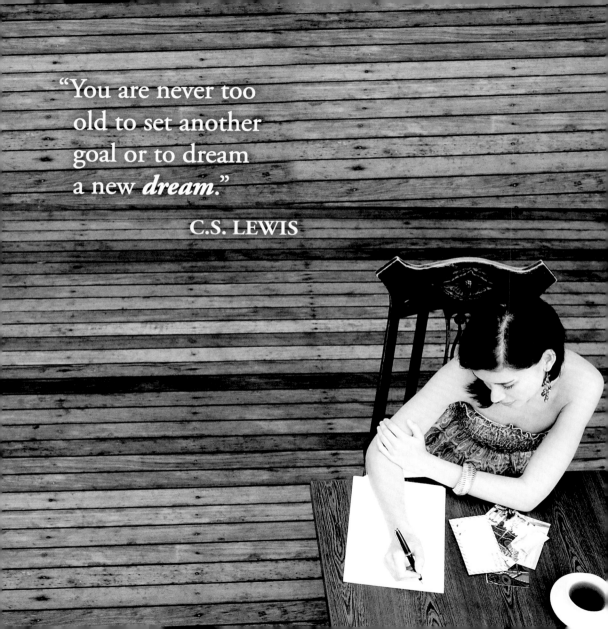

"You are never too old to set another goal or to dream a new *dream*."

C.S. LEWIS

365 Days of Purpose

A FEW YEARS AGO I was frustrated. I was staring down a new year, a new decade, and my fortieth birthday, and I hadn't yet become the person I wanted to be when I grew up. I have a beautiful family—a husband and two sons whom I love dearly—and a successful business and many other blessings in my life, for which I am so grateful, but my own personal goal had always been to be a "real" writer—and I hadn't accomplished that yet.

Several years of off-and-on (more off than on) journaling and half-hearted free writing had left me with a pile of unfinished, neglected stories and essays. My passion is to connect with others through my writing, and I just wasn't doing that in a significant way. I was depressed about this and disappointed in myself. Also during this time, people whom I don't consider "real" writers—people like Paris Hilton, for example—were publishing books that landed on bestseller lists, and that just made me angry. Nothing against Paris Hilton—obviously she has been hugely successful in marketing her particular brand to a particular fan base, and good for her—but I know for a fact that she is not a better writer than I am. What the heck was wrong with me?

I wasn't yet sure what shape becoming a real writer would take, but I decided that in order to get better at my craft and figure it all out, I needed to adopt a daily discipline that would force me to write. I also needed to defeat, or at least write my way around, my harsh inner editor, so to speak. I could blame my lack of writing initiative on the busy-ness of life, but most often, the truth was that I didn't want to write poorly, so I just didn't write. To that end, I hogtied my inner perfectionist and stuffed her in the utility room, behind the cat litter box and HVAC equipment. Ha!

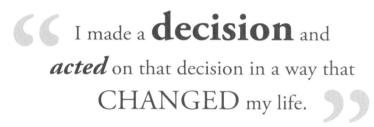

I made a **decision** and *acted* on that decision in a way that CHANGED my life.

But what could I do to develop a daily writing discipline, a commitment that would help me become a better writer and serve as a springboard for new projects? I remembered my sister, Jeannie, once telling me about a writing course she took in college, in which the students were required to write a poem a day for a month. I seized upon this regimen as a way to practice writing every day, like journaling, but with more structure. I decided to jumpstart my practice by writing a poem a day, for the month of January. It could be a terrible poem, a homely, unpolished poem, an unoriginal poem—it didn't matter. I just had to write one every day.

I ran the idea by my dear friend, Jennifer Anderson, a gifted writer whose work I admire. She was encouraging, as she always is, and told me via email that she thought the poem-a-day exercise was a great one, and had I seen *Julie & Julia*? I should write a poem a day for a year, taking it on as a transformative discipline, and blog about it! I thought, *Wow. That sounds really hard.* But I knew it would be good for me. The blog would require accountability on my part, and even if I had only a few readers following my progress, I would have to do what I said I would.

Jennifer's final note on the poem-a-day discipline helped me make up my mind:

"Hi Sarah--Can you imagine if you did that and had 365 poems--or pages--after a year? I can't advise you about blogging, though. Imagine if you did it and hated the pressure or the lack of privacy? But I am captivated by your idea of transformative disciplines! Love, Jen"

I decided I really wanted those 365 poems—or pages—and the pressure and lack of privacy were probably what I needed to get them.

Another thing: Besides using my daily poetry discipline as a way to develop a work habit, I saw it as a way to pay closer attention to my life, to heighten my awareness that every day—even the ones in which not much seems to happen—is a once-in-a-lifetime deal, and therefore, valuable.

I had picked up Michael Chabon's *Manhood for Amateurs*—which really isn't just for men. I was particularly moved by his essays on fatherhood. In his chapter "The Memory Hole," he talks about all the drawings and art projects his four children bring home from school and how they are so numerous that he and his wife don't know what to do with them, other than throw them away. He goes on to say, "The truth is that in every way, I am squandering the treasure of my life. It's not that I don't take enough pictures, though I don't, or that I don't keep a diary, though iCal and my monthly

Visa bill are the closest I come to a thoughtful prose record of events. Every day is like a kid's drawing, offered to you with a strange mixture of ceremoniousness and offhand disregard, yours for the keeping. Some of the days are rich and complicated, others inscrutable, others little more than a stray gray mark on a ragged page. Some you manage to hang on to, though your reasons for doing so are often hard to fathom. But most of them you just ball up and throw away."

When I read this, I realized that I had balled up and thrown away so many days. Too often, I had failed to see the poetry in the rhythms of my life; the beauty in the "rich, complicated days," as well as the "stray gray marks." Chabon's essay made me wish for a meaningful way to document these days, a way to recognize and receive the time I've been given with more awareness and appreciation.

After considering Chabon's words, I turned to a favorite devotional, a compilation of writings by Frederick Buechner. In a meditation titled, "Life Itself is Grace," he says, "Listen to your life. See it for the fathomless mystery that it is. In the boredom and pain of it no less than in the excitement and gladness: touch, taste, smell your way to the holy and hidden heart of it because in the last analysis all moments are key moments, and life itself is grace."

And what happened after I decided to write 365 poems in 365 days? Well, I did it! In addition to forcing myself to write daily and develop a "real" writer's work habit, I ended up with a valuable body of work and a whole bunch of friends and supporters who were reading my work and cheering me on. After a year's time, I had enough good poems to make an entire book—which I'm finishing up now and will send to print soon. I also started working on another book, a memoir, which I'm really excited about. My poetry blog was picked up by OCinsite, a media conglomerate that owns our local newspaper and several magazines. And I was recently asked by a friend who teaches third grade to speak to her class for their poetry unit, which was an absolute joy and one of the highlights of my entire year.

To summarize, I made a decision and acted on that decision in a way that changed my life. My poem-a-day practice helped me take steps toward becoming a "real" writer with two books in the works. Even more than that, I learned to listen to my life. To frame my days instead of balling them up and throwing them away. And to remember that all moments are key moments, and life itself is grace. DM

SARAH VANDERVEEN

"Perhaps all the dragons in our lives are princesses who are only waiting to see us act, just once, with beauty and *courage*. Perhaps everything that frightens us is, in its deepest essence, something helpless that wants our LOVE."

RAINER MARIA RILKE

SPEAKING INTO EXISTENCE

My Forgiveness

I WAS IN THE BATHROOM in my parent's house—a place my heart never felt to be home. I was crying, muffled sobs so my mother couldn't hear me. Outside of the room, I could hear my family celebrating my sister's 2011 high school graduation and her newfound acceptance into a university.

My sobs were getting louder. I couldn't help it. Everything was pouring out of me— snot, salt, sweat, and so much pain. Alarmingly, I knew it had nothing to do with just finding out I was kicked out of law school.

In 2009, my parents had disowned me. "You are no longer my daughter," my father told me. I could handle that. I knew I *could* live without them. "You are forbidden to speak to your sisters." It was those words that woke me up in tears every night for the next year.

It's 2012 now, and my parents have since "re-owned" me—I guess that's what you call it. But up until that moment—sitting on the cold Turkish marble tile my mother had imported, my tears stinging and eyes puffy –I hadn't forgiven them for what they had done to me.

All four of us, my sisters and I, were raised to live on the border in between worlds—

not intentionally, of course, but we were nevertheless split—in language, culture, dress, and even in demeanor. At home, we were Iraqi girls, going to church, speaking our native Chaldean Neo-Aramaic dialect, studying diligently without play, and certainly not acting like "American" girls. At school, we chattered in English to our friends about things ranging from biology and math, to clothes and boys. But we never entertained the possibility of wearing a mini skirt, like Lily in math class, or going to the movies with friends on the weekend, much less eventually dating *before* we got married.

Sure, today we've turned out to be healthy, *almost*-well-adjusted women with various professional degrees and passions for changing the world, and we've even developed newer lines of communication with our parents. But in all the old skins we shed, there is a layered, intricate story.

Of course, I cannot speak for my sisters, as I hold our conversations of past and present sacred. I can speak for myself and the webs I had intricately woven to keep up with both worlds as we were growing up… In fact, I had spun with such fervor from my teenage years up until my young-adulthood that I had suddenly become lost in the once orderly-patterned lies.

To be honest (ha, finally!), I lied to my parents…about everything. I had become accustomed to dealing with them using convenient non-truths, so when I started lying about my current life partner, it was all part of the routine.

Simple questions from my mother like "Why didn't you answer my call" required only simple answers: "I was studying, I fell asleep, I forgot" and, of course, "I am sorry, it won't happen again."

But it did happen again—and again, and again, for the first year and a half of my relationship with my partner. I had nightmares about them finding out. Awake, I tortured myself, daydreaming that they'd found out he was Muslim. I shuddered at the thought of the conversation. Then one day I couldn't do it anymore.

It might have been a combination of guilt and the suffocating tightness that grasped my heart and throat every time I hid Mahdi from my parents or anyone that might reveal him to my parents, but I woke one day knowing "today was the day." I had to tell them.

It wasn't an epiphany that suddenly empowered me and eliminated the crippling fear I constantly felt when telling my parents anything that meant gaining my agency. I wish. Instead, it was the sheer exhaustion of hiding, running, and covering my tracks, making sure one story built upon another. I knew my Jenga-tower was falling. Literally, my physical body was failing.

Mahdi, on the other hand, was not moved by my parents' intolerance for him. Day in and day out, he reassured me that their reaction might be what I predicted, but that it also might not be—it might be different, forgiving, embracing. I was too busy speaking into existence what I expected from them to hear him. I went forth with fear in my heart, and perhaps a sliver of hope, which faded as I told them my secret. As I predicted, my confession ended in misery. My mom's numerous daily phone calls suddenly ended. My sisters' emails, smiley texts, phone calls, and visits ceased, as well. Even the financial pools my parents provided me dried up.

In my loss, I also gained. Speaking my truth gave me something I never had in my life—ownership of myself, my self-worth, and control over what I could speak into existence. But the gain came only after experiencing various stages of grief.

Reflecting on my journey, I have come to realize that, yes, my grief is healing but my journey of empowerment has become everlasting. However, at every stage of grief, I believed that my journey had ended. "That's it, Cynthia! That's all you have left." My stage of *denial* happened the *day after* being disowned. I felt like a bird that had finally leapt from the highest mountain to soar. "I did it! I finally told them the truth! Who cares if they don't want me as a daughter? I got this—I don't want your love or financial weights on me!" But my soaring fell short when I realized I did not know how to flap my wings, much less how to navigate through the new world that had manifested.

In my frantic attempts to gain speed, I fell into a vicious tag-team between the second and third stages of grief: anger and bargaining. Inwardly, I battled over what I should have said to them. My anger was reflected in the way I treated others around me. I was bitter, which was often uncalled for and new for me. The woman serving my coffee, the students I tutored, even my own partner could not speak the words I wanted to hear. The anger was growing into a tumor and becoming unbearable. The only way to alleviate the pain was to bargain with my ego. "If I did it over again, I would have said nothing. It wasn't so bad keeping this from them…I blew it out of proportion in my head…This is my fault…"

I had reached the stage that felt the most familiar to me, the *guilty* story I always told myself in my relationship with my parents. "It's my fault," even when I knew somewhere in my core that wasn't true. I had convinced myself that this time they were at fault, because losing my sisters in the process was both unwarranted and paralyzing.

I've heard that after running the first ten miles of a marathon, it is your mind that carries you through to the end. You have to convince yourself that you can run the next mile, and the next, and the next. That's what I did. I ran. I hit auto-pilot and sprinted through two full-time jobs, a full-time school schedule, practice entrance exams for law school, law school applications, and even a network-marketing business I had started in 2009. I didn't stop. I couldn't stop. *What would happen if I did?* I feared my heart might stop from the overwhelming pain I could not contain; it was seeping into my clothes, my hair, my veins.

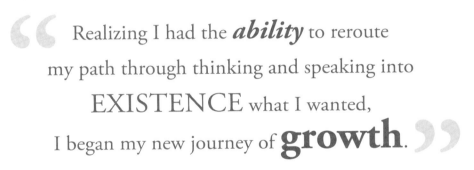

Realizing I had the *ability* to reroute my path through thinking and speaking into EXISTENCE what I wanted, I began my new journey of **growth**.

I don't think I realized when I stopped running, but when I did, I was gasping for air for a long time. My anger had become sadness, but my depression was masked. No one besides those who saw my blood-shot eyes knew just how unhappy I was. Emptiness enveloped me, startling me whenever I felt any kind of uplifting contentment or happiness. I desperately tried to hold on tight to it whenever it came near, but it was temporary and superficial.

However, this story is about overcoming and becoming, not drowning. I had leapt and had faith that there would be a net to catch me, and indeed there was. My parents' reaction was not surprising, but my choice to react the way I did, letting my spirit unravel in my hands, was my choice. Let me explain.

Today, I live a completely different life. I live my life by design, and not by default. But this did not happen overnight. It evolved in much the same way as a masterpiece—by consistent daily activity, so-called "slight-edge" actions. I learned about the formation of habit. We all have habits, but we are not always aware of them. There are habits of communication with various people, habits of studying, eating, sleeping, living! However, I had not been aware of the process in which habit was formed both consciously and subconsciously. In fact, when I finally stepped back a year or so later to evaluate my stages of grief (from the stages of acceptance and forgiveness), I was startled to find that my subconscious slight-edge actions of "unhappiness" had led me to my intense search for my former internal joy. The same principles behind the positive slight-edge thinking and actions that had elevated me to become a law student, a scholar, an activist, and a leader in so many sectors of my life were also behind the negative slight-edge moves that created small destructions that led to an overall picture of sadness.

The only valuable piece of information that I retained from my brief tenure in law school was that in order to succeed, I had to change the way I thought about approaching and solving problems and even how I wrote and analyzed issues. What law school (and quite frankly, the entirety of my formal education) failed to highlight was that our thoughts are actually things! Today, thanks to discovering the amazing compendium of knowledge delegated to Quantum Physics, I don't sound obscenely out of my mind when I say, yes, indeed, what you truly think and speak will be.

Realizing I had the ability to reroute my path through thinking and speaking into existence what I wanted, I began my new journey of growth. I watched and read anything and everything related to my thoughts becoming things, and learned about my energy and how my energy flowed through everything and everyone. I practiced transforming my thoughts and attention from what I didn't want to what I did want. I reframed simple thoughts like, "I hope it doesn't rain," to "I hope it is sunny and warm today." I worked on centering myself by practicing what renowned physician and world-leader in Mind Body Medicine Deepak Chopra coined as *The Law of Least Effort*.

This Law meant that I had to *accept* myself as being disowned by making a commitment to accept all people, situations, circumstances, and events as they occurred in that moment of my disownment. I could wish for things in the future to be different with my family, but in the moment, I had to accept them as they were and design my life in the present without them. I also had to take *responsibility*, but not in the "I'm right and you're wrong" sense of responsibility (although at times I would have liked to leave it at that). Doctor Chopra defined responsibility as "not blaming anyone or anything for your situation, including yourself." Instead of wasting energy on blaming, I worked on seeing the life-forms of opportunity that these perceived problems contained – a tactic also clarified and taught to me by Napoleon Hill, as I delved deeper into my self-imposed self-education.

Perhaps most difficult to apply on a daily, habitual basis was being *defenseless*. This third aspect of *The Law of Least Effort* teaches that when we are able to let go of any need or desire to defend ourselves or our personal perspectives – even just to state them – there is no longer any reason to fight or argue about those perspectives. With all of these tools, I shaped and designed my thoughts; and in return, I saw the manifestations come alive. I came to an inner understanding that I could not (and should not) control my parents' behavior. A year ago, had I chosen to learn these very concepts of the Universe, I might not have written the first part of this story – I wouldn't have anything to write. But alas, I have learned that the Universe's timing is impeccable.

One year after my disownment, I had been accepted to law school in California, and my mom had left me a voicemail when I had least expected it, when I had finally learned to stop crying… This time, I was prepared, but I was scared. In all of my morning affirmations, statements of gratitude, and meditations visualizing the health, wealth, and happiness, I wanted, I had never addressed actually forgiving my parents for the grief they had caused. I had, however, envisioned us in conversation; perhaps, I assumed that if we had reached that state of reconnection, I would have thusly forgiven them.

But in my heart and my core, I did not believe I had reached a state of forgiveness with my parents. Reconnecting with my family, hugging, kissing, and holding my sisters, was emotional. My heart had cracked and poured wide open. When the zenith of intensity had passed and my mother asked for an apology for my "behavior," old anger began to creep back. I mourned the year I missed without my sisters, but I wasn't about to retreat to a past I had worked so hard to redesign.

What I had struggled to hold onto for so long, a stitch of my old self, being in law school, and even more, clinging to the belief that my parents were wrong, hurtful, and cruel, was all obsolete at this moment when *I had everything in my life*, including my family. I had to stop poisoning my abundant, flowing river when it was finally clearing and I could see my reflection. I had to forgive my parents, for myself. I had to stop struggling with the idea that forgiving meant giving up. I hadn't lost. Quite the contrary—that day, after learning I'd failed out of law school, I leaned against the bathroom wall and I forgave. I forgave my parents so I could love them the way I had spoken and envisioned I could. DM

CYNTHIA LUOIS

THE ROAD TO *PARADISE* IS PAVED

With Good Intentions, Too

"**T**O HELL WITH GOOD INTENTIONS.**" Illich's words rang in my head as I read over the pre-field materials for the Students for International Change (currently Support for International Change, www.sichange.org) project with which I had chosen to assist in East-Central Africa during May through July of 2006. The common adage "The road to Hell is paved with good intentions" may have some merit to it, as well, depending on one's perspective. But I'm not sure I had encountered either version, up until then in that room at the University of Arizona in 2006. "*To Hell with good intentions…*" Those words spoke to me, and not only because I was in agreement with much of what Illich related in his piece. Those words and the content of that article gave me pause because they guided me to reflect on and consider how I had been living my own life up to that point. Ultimately, they also provided me with moments of insight before, during, and after my service-trip abroad. Those moments and the points I share with you, the reader, are really less about the trip and more about my realization of the power of intention – which was not an instantaneous event. The trip, in this regard, simply served as the pretext for the discovery. The trip was the catalyst to my learning over these past five years about the power of intention, not only in my life, but in the lives of all people. I *intend* here, to share my experience earned, and my lessons learned (yes, you can insert a smiley-face here). The secondary intention being that you may – if you so choose – maximize the utility of such power in your own authentic way, to enjoy a genuine life by design, with optimal quality.

Back to my initial epiphany then: In that moment, reading over the pre-field preparation article on the ethics of international service-work, I looked inward at what "good intentions" meant to me. My own moral code of conduct, deeply rooted in my extraordinarily strong religious upbringing as a Shi'a Muslim, typically had me peacefully reconcile my thoughts and deeds with myself as long as "my *intentions were good.*" Illich's words spoke to something inside of me that reminded me how important my intentions were to me in anything I did. More pragmatically, I realized I'd better have a *damn good* reason to even *want* to go to a country like Tanzania to teach adults and children about the HIV pandemic that was (and unfortunately, still is) disproportionately affecting them (and generally all of the world's poorest populations). Who the Hell did I think I was? A benevolent do-gooder? That simply was not going to be enough. More importantly, such naïve thinking would certainly be *completely inappropriate.*

So, I was in a quandary. My whole life was (and still is) guided by my intentions and how I asserted them to myself, but in that present-moment, I faced figuring out how to make my intentions *matter* for what most people would generally agree to be a life-altering experience in and of itself—volunteering in a developing country. Given the scope of the world's extreme poverty problem and the multiple issues – sexism, racism, classism – that are simultaneously at its root while also intersecting it, what did I think I could do? And what did it even matter what I thought, whether in the form of an intention or otherwise? I was just one person – one *kid*. A kid just finishing college as a pre-med, who thought maybe he knew something about the world after reading a few books about righteous medical doctors in the field, a few articles on international development and public health, and was now getting some "experience" working with a non-governmental, not-for-profit organization. How was I to reconcile what I was getting myself into? And what would I do with myself afterward?

In retrospect, I know I definitely thought I was smarter and more capable than I really was. But to my credit, and in no self-righteous or self-aggrandizing terms, I was more aware and more experienced than most people I knew (read: with whom I interacted), regarding issues of social justice. I knew this simply by comparing viewpoints: mine, theirs, and those of the scholars whose work I devoured in my search for answers on what to do and where to start.

Ironically, I was actually pessimistic about the work of major organizations that fell into the same category as SIC. I had a strong distrust for many global groups – I still distrust many of them, to some extent, for many reasons – including certain sections of the U.N., essentially the whole of the World Bank, the International Monetary Fund, some multinational private corporations, and even quite a few international non-profits. I don't feel compelled to elaborate my reasons why, here. What I want to point out is that I understood that righteous, philanthropic causes should not nourish the systematic, global cycle of oppression in our world that is unfortunately normally "addressed" with false charitable gestures (and that's what they are, when by nature of the charity or aide, another segment of our global society is going underserved. For some insight, the reader is referred to the works of Paulo Freire, John Perkins,

Paul Farmer, and James Orbinski, among other poignant and opinionated authors). Despite my pessimism, I felt I had to do something. Though I realized that Illich was right, I understood I wasn't necessarily supposed to throw my intentions out the window. On the contrary, I realized I had to get even more laser-focused and crystal-clear on my intentions and their power to drive me.

> " The power in my calculated
> INTENTIONS will lead me to attract
> whatever I need
> and *manifest* exactly what I want,
> just as it has done so throughout the
> whole of my **life**. "

I made myself take a step back and even *put intent into my intentions* themselves. At that point, I made a personal resolution. I resolved (in this case, placed intent in an intention) to do my work while always cognizant that it could only truly be "good" while my motive (the intention in which the resolution was placed) remained to bring preferential quality of life to all people, as much as I physically and possibly could. Now, whether right or wrong (a subjective matter), the ideal course of action, to me, was to create what I wanted for myself and do my part to enable others to create what they wanted for themselves. I *intended* to always care and do my best to be decisive about what to do next. I actually phrased it much more negatively in my mind at the time – I aimed to "prevent" myself from "falling into apathy and ambivalence." I've since learned to think and speak what I want, and not what I do not want, to exploit the Law of Attraction (something else my intentions have since brought me to learn more about and utilize) to my will. At any rate, what I put out into the world back then in 2006 was a defining intention, just the same.

I *intended* to start and maintain a lifestyle of service in elevating the quality of life of others. Side-note: Near the end of my service-trip, I learned I was accepted to medical school, and that "lifestyle of service" bit made it on to the mission-statement of my entering class, *because of me*. Go see it the next time you're at the Arizona Health Sciences Center in Tucson, Class of 2010, on the wall outside the College of Medicine Admissions Office. It is evidence that I effectively influenced the minds, attitudes, and intentions of over 100 other pillars of civil society (doctors are great, aren't they?), *with my own, one, powerful intention*. Now, back to my monologue… For some reason, I wanted to launch my personal journey with action and an experience I thought would permanently keep me on my path. I wanted to begin with people in some of the most dire states of need. I don't know why, but it was part of my *intent*. I wanted to give a hand-up to people directly affected by a deadly disease, made deadlier by its spread through some of the poorest regions on Earth.

Marrying myself to my overall intention – to always care, decisively act, and provide what could be objectively measured as *true help* – defined my productivity and my own sense of achievement during my trip. This is not the place for me to elaborate on a complete and detailed recount of my experiences in Tanzania, but I will say that before embarking, I actively *intended* to design and create an experience for myself and the other volunteers, to ensure that the group's work would be exemplary and conducive to true and real solutions to the abject poverty and disproportionate suffering of people we were to encounter in the field.

And it worked perfectly... almost... sometimes. Again, I was young. We were all young. We had a strong sense of idealism. I know that I also hadn't broken out of my pattern of relying more on myself, rather than leveraging the skills and talents of others at every opportunity. Another intention that currently guides my work is to be mindful of what others can contribute and leverage them at any and every chance I get. I do not have to (nor do I want to) do everything on my own.

Was my worldview enhanced by my first service-trip to a developing region? Of course. Do I understand that, at the end of the day, all people simply want to be happy? Certainly. These are the typical consequential experiences of most international volunteers whose work takes them to low socio-economic-status regions. But most importantly, I realized that I had developed and grown as a human being before, during, and after my trip. Specifically, I came to a perspective seeing and respecting myself in a position to offer certain things to the world to enable progress and bring more and more people together, over and over again, to do the same. To me, that's the key: power in numbers. And that realization manifested as a direct result of my actions that were driven by my original, powerful *intention*. My intention guided me to the vantage point I have now, to look at power dynamics in our world and not only realize immediately that power lies within groups that can organize themselves most

effectively, rally together, and add to their movements – but to also see in myself the power to create revolutionary movements.

Power in numbers is the whole basis for teams, campaigns, political parties, and tribes (I think Seth Godin would agree; Google his TED talk). Once people show up, and do so consistently, all the needed resources – whether material, financial, or even more people – inevitably and naturally manifest. Additionally, we can all relate stories – good, bad, or otherwise – of what can be created by the power of thousands of people working together with a common goal. I now know that I have all of the ingredients to structure new ideas, assemble new teams, and develop new programs conducive to my original defining intention, all the while effectively drawing on the power of intention, again. Side-note: Notice how my intentions have brought me to also understand the power of clear, specific affirmations. More examples, that also effectively end this paragraph: The power in my calculated intentions will lead me to attract whatever I need and manifest exactly what I want, just as it has done so throughout the whole of my life. That power is what I personally leverage to create movements that progressively succeed at quality of life optimization for all people around the world.

That last point is impactful to me because it proves another realization I had that, again, many people with similar international experiences to mine generally conclude. When we build our communities up with like-minded people who can bring different talents, skills, and experiences to the table, we manifest the truth that the locus of control to guide and shape any circumstances in our world lies within – not without. I've realized with my defining moment that the locus of control residing in each person can and should be empowered with an intelligent, thought-out intention. If and when we finally manage to assemble each of our teams, each of us knowing exactly who we are, what we stand for, and what we have to offer – in other words, when we each intimately know the core within each of ourselves – we will all be playing the right positions on this team called "humanity," and we will collectively achieve goals for our society that will literally astound us.

> " STEP into your
> **greatness**,
> and be great.
> *Intend* it. "

It is my hope and prayer that we do not end up wondering what took us so long. In fact, I am placing a new intention here and into the world right now: I intend that you and I, in our own authentic and unique ways, succeed in inspiring and bringing diverse groups of people together to contribute to communities, and effect *truly* positive change in our world, *enhancing quality of life for all people.* I am excited to see what we will manifest. Step into your authentic personality—your purpose for being. Step into your greatness, and be great. *Intend* it. DM

DR. MOHAMMAD MAHDI PESSARAKLI, M.D.

One Day at a Time

I FOUND DAD ASLEEP with his head down on his desk. I noticed his cigarette ash was almost as long as the cigarette that used to be there. It was pitch dark and freezing in his office in the garage. As I stood there that November night in 2008, it was so cold I could see my breath.

I was spending the Thanksgiving holiday at my parents' home in Albuquerque with my three-year-old son, Caden, and my husband, Michael. Living in San Diego, we weren't able to see them as often as we would have liked, so we treasured the time we could share with them.

Finding my father like this seemed odd. The holidays were usually a jubilant time in my parents' home. I felt a little concerned and wondered if something was troubling him.

I discussed the disturbing scene with my mom. She made light of it—as she often did when there were things she didn't want to discuss—and changed the subject.

A Troubling Discovery

I began to notice stacks of unopened bills in different places in the house—the kitchen, my parents' bedroom, my dad's office. *Strange.*

I asked my mom about their financial condition. She was vague and changed the subject, *again*. Investigating a pile of bills in her bedroom, I noticed a cable statement notifying them of disconnection if the bill—three months overdue—wasn't paid by the end of the month. Now I feared the situation was serious. Dad had always complained about not having enough money and about the spending habits of me, my mom, and my sister. I usually didn't give much thought to his comments because we always had enough. In fact, we lived an amazingly blessed life, enjoying private education, dinners out, traveling to beautiful places, dance lessons, nice clothes, and studying abroad.

I pulled myself out of the privileged trailer that was my childhood into present reality. Mom told me not to worry; everything would be fine.

We managed to get through the holiday, but underneath the surface, something terrible seemed to be looming. I took the cable bill with me when we left and paid it. It was one small thing my husband and I could do to help.

A Sudden Crisis

After learning that my sister and her husband had paid for my parents' Christmas tree, I realized things were *not* getting better.

Out of nowhere, in March my sister had a stroke. My mom was visiting me in San Diego at the time. We couldn't fly out until the next morning and didn't know if my sister would make it through the night. We felt helpless. My brother-in-law, Kevin, was freaking out. He and my sister had been together since high school. They were each other's other half, and she meant everything to him. When my mom and I finally landed and were able to get into the ICU, we saw my sister, full of probes and needles, wearing an oxygen mask. Feeling even more helpless, we started to cry. Days later, my sister had a seizure, which was one of the scariest things I'd ever witnessed. Damn it! Why hadn't the nurse given her enough anti-seizure medicine? We felt powerless, frustrated, and angry. I prayed:

God, please help her get through this. Are you sending us a message about what matters most in life?

During the following week, we alternated days at the hospital so my sister was never alone. Kevin spent every night there.

I noticed my parents never said a word about their situation and how serious their financial condition had become. They always put my sister and her well-being first. Looking back, it's amazing they could do this, knowing the floor was cracking beneath them. It came as no surprise, though, because my parents had *always* put my sister and me first.

I had my dad's car cleaned and his brakes fixed. I was happy I could do this for him and knew he appreciated it. I'm sure it was a little awkward, though, given that he'd been the family provider up until that time, rarely needing help from others.

By the grace of God, we didn't lose my sister and she completely recovered.

The Road to Nowhere
Later that spring, I wrote my parents a letter to let them know how much my sister and I—and our respective families—loved and supported them. However, it was time they made critical decisions regarding their finances. I asked them where they were going and what they were doing to handle their situation. They needed to stop sticking their

heads in the sand, face reality, and do something.

I was frustrated with them but also really worried. Were they going to become homeless? Were they going to have enough money to eat? Struggling to make our own ends meet, what could my husband and I do to help them? My parents had taken care of my sister and me our whole lives. I felt guilty, knowing that the privileges they'd given us had likely contributed to their current situation. I felt powerless because I didn't have the financial means to fix it.

> " Too often, we only hear about the *ugliness* in people, the selfishness. Yet, in this GESTURE, we experienced another example of the **beauty** in other people. "

I encouraged them to consider bankruptcy. I later found out that wasn't an option, given my dad's professional obligations. I knew losing their house would devastate them— especially my mom, who had spent so much time renovating and decorating it. Their house had always been a place of laughter and generosity. My parents loved to entertain. I hoped they would be able to let the house go. Foreclosure was inevitable—

no longer an "if" but a "when."

I enclosed a little money in my letter and told them, "I love you. Now get after it! You can handle this! You are the strongest people I know."

The End of an Era

By December 2009, my parents had borrowed money where they could and had done everything possible to prevent their house from falling into foreclosure. My parents' friends lent them money, and their generosity was remarkable, but it wasn't enough to prevent the inevitable. I found out later that part of the problem was that my dad's small business, a law partnership, wasn't doing well. Unfortunately, no business was doing well at the time due to the economic crisis gripping the nation. Many businesses closed or were on the verge of closing.

My husband, son, and I spent Christmas with my parents that year. I was pregnant and knew this was going to be the last Christmas I would spend in my childhood house—a house once belonging to my grandmother, who died when I was eight. I had 36 years of memories in that house—36 years of the same Christmas routine: A big Christmas Eve party, including a formal sit-down dinner with family and friends. Dad—always a little tipsy from Mom's eggnog—would dress up as Santa. Luminaries would line the yard. My sister and I would wear matching pajamas and gaze at the Christmas tree and the lights reflecting off the ten-foot windows encasing the living room. It was magical in so many ways, but what I remember most was the magic of being with my family. The smiles, the laughter, the hugs. Those are the moments I will hold onto and cherish the rest of my life.

I emptied out my bedroom before I flew back. When I left the house, it was like saying goodbye to an old friend.

At the airport on the way home, I felt heartbroken. I hated seeing my amazing, beautiful, giving, loving parents struggling. I wished I had enough money to get their house out of foreclosure or buy them a new one.

By the spring of 2010, it was official the house was gone and they needed to move.

The First Miracle

Just when things seemed hopeless, some fellow Rotarians offered for my parents to live rent free in their home for a year. It was an act of generosity usually only seen in old movies or on the best reruns of "Little House on the Prairie." We were amazed. I thanked the Lord for sending my parents two guardian angels who gave them a safe, warm, and loving place to lay their heads for awhile. They just needed a break and some time to get things back on track—a hand up versus a hand out. This was the miracle we had prayed for.

So, late that summer, my parents, both in their mid-sixties, found themselves moving everything they owned to the Rotarians' house in Los Lunas, 45 minutes away. I couldn't fly out to help them due to the arrival of my little girl, Addison, weeks earlier. Thankfully, my sister, her husband, my aunt and uncle, and their friends helped my parents with the slow and painful move. My dad wasn't helping. He was depressed and in deep denial. A friend and former law partner had a frank conversation with him, telling him it was time to move on. Dad finally pulled himself together and helped with the move.

Another Crisis, Another Miracle

Then, in the spring of 2011, the owners put the house up for sale. My parents knew of the owner's plans when they moved in, but in light of the current economic climate, felt it would take at least a year for the house to sell. No such luck. The house sold in three months. My parents were going to have to move again at the end of the summer. All of the old feelings of panic resurfaced, and I wondered what my parents were going to do. Where were they going to live?

Under the weight of all of this chaos and stress, my dad ended up in the emergency room. He had suffered a heart attack. I flew out, and a rerun of my sister's hospital experience unfolded. We spent long days in the hospital, felt helpless, and didn't know if my dad was going to make it. Damn it! Why hadn't he taken better care of himself? Again, we felt powerless, frustrated, and angry. I prayed to God once more:

Help my dad get through this. Are you sending us another message about what matters most in life?

" I **choose** to wake up every day
and PERSEVERE,
regardless of what may appear to be
dire or *desperate* circumstances. "

161

"You will never do anything in this world without **courage**. It is the greatest quality of the mind next to honor."

ARISTOTLE

The thought of losing him was overwhelming. He'd been my hero my whole life; the person I looked up to most. What would I do without him? Thankfully, my dad survived.

After the medical drama, we had to switch gears and get my parents moved again. Dad was even more fragile this time. He really couldn't help with much. I could only provide support long distance, due to my own family obligations and commitments. The daunting questions surfaced again. Where were they going to go? What could they afford? What was going to happen to them?

At that point, God sent two more guardian angels. Two of my mom's clients invited my parents to move into their beautiful home in one of the nicest neighborhoods in Albuquerque for a monthly rent they could afford. We couldn't believe it! We were amazed by their generosity. Too often, we only hear about the ugliness in people— the road rage, the get-out-of-my-way attitude, the selfishness. Yet, in this gesture, we experienced another example of the beauty in other people.

A *Third Miracle*
By the end of that summer, my parents were tired, but thankfully my sister had recovered, my dad was alive, and my parents were in another stable environment. Life slowed down and gave them a much needed rest.

But then two months after my parents moved in, the homeowners were given an opportunity to sell their home that they couldn't pass up. It was a blessing, considering their house had been on the market for four years. My parents were thrilled for them, but devastated by the news.

They needed to move—*again!* All the old feelings of panic resurfaced. Again, I wondered where they were going to go. What could they afford? What was going to happen to them? Could my parents emotionally and physically endure this chaos again? My heart sank. Just when the skies had cleared, another storm was bearing down on top of them. They were beginning to feel hopeless. So was I.

My dad's business hadn't improved, and the homes they could afford to rent were, according to my mom, just awful. She, the pillar that had been keeping my parents together, started to crack. Leroy, my dad's dog and best friend, was going to have to be given away. My parents were becoming more and more depressed, and time was not on their side.

Then, out of the blue, the realtor who sold the home my parents were living in called to let them know that the owners of a home two doors down were looking for renters and were willing to rent the house at a price my parents could afford. Unbelievable—a third miracle! God had sent yet another set of guardian angels to help my parents as they continued to work their way through their financial crisis.

Through It All, a Defining Moment

It's almost impossible to express my thanks to the three couples who ensured that my parents would have a roof over their heads. Words aren't big enough and can't say thank you enough for their generosity. The actions they took were defining moments in my parents' lives. I love these guardian angels for what they did for my parents and my family. The fact that the world still has people like them in it gives me hope for our children's futures.

I'm also in awe of my parents' determination to wake up every day and make their situation better. Dad's commitment to his law firm, his employees, and his clients is remarkable, considering that he and his partner typically don't get a paycheck. Keeping the doors open and making payroll are their priorities. My mom's strength—not only for herself, but also for my dad—is astounding. She has taken on so much and continues to look forward to the future. Most couples wouldn't survive what my parents have been through, yet neither of them blames the other for their situation. They turned to each other for strength and resolved to get through the situation together. They are inspiring role models to me.

My parents' actions through this horrible experience have become a defining moment in my life. I've seen what matters most:

Faith, Family, Friends, and Service

I am more grateful for what I have and not so focused on what I don't have. I have slowed down and appreciate the time I *do* have with my family and friends. I am grateful my sister and my dad are still with me. I'm grateful my family, my husband, and his family have been able to provide support during this difficult time. I am grateful my parents are still together and aren't homeless. I am grateful for their undying determination and hard-working spirit. I am grateful I am my parents' daughter. I am so proud of them. I'm even more resolved to overcome challenges and obstacles in my life. I choose to wake up every day and persevere, regardless of what may appear to be dire or desperate circumstances.

Most importantly, if I can help someone, I will. I will do it because it's the right thing to do, not because I expect something in return. Who knows? My actions might become a defining moment in someone else's life. DM

KARLA J. PINCKES

The Happy Bubble

I T WAS THE GNARLIEST days of my life. There I was, sobbing in bed for two, now three days. The intense magnitude of my reality had completely crushed me this time. "Will I ever be okay? How did I let this happen? What am I going to do?!" Insane pain, depression, uncontrollable anxiety, confusion, frustration, fear…I had it all.

I had just escaped from an abusive (one-year) marriage and was hiding out in Durham, NC, close to one of my best girlfriends who loved, supported, and protected me the best she could. I had been introduced to an osteopath doctor, who insisted that Prolotherapy injections would heal my soft-tissue injuries, from torn ligaments to herniated discs; this was my winning lotto ticket. It's a natural amino acid complex in a saline solution, not another narcotic or steroid, so I trusted the doctor's expertise and recommendation. Some 300 injections later, I was paralyzed with what felt like fire spiders and flaming ninja stars ripping through me with each pulse. "My poor body…I'm so sorry!" I cried as I attempted to hug myself. I thought I was being tough by not taking any pain meds for the injections, but now I wish I had. I had detoxed myself off the pills and didn't want to go back, especially not after the side effects they caused, like kidney stones, hair loss, migraines and partial liver failure.

My 30-year-old body had been traumatized too many times, one ridiculous injury, illness, or accident after another, and now I was mentally and emotionally broken, too. The last thing I would do was call my family and tell them the mess I was in—besides, they're 3,000 miles away, and there was no way I could admit to needing help. Praying to the Universal Divine Intelligence, my higher Self, and all the Angels was all I could do in this total meltdown. So I fiercely demanded, "Really?! Why?!…show me, tell me, I need an answer!" again and again. Why was I living out this karmic joke? I closed my tear-flooded eyes to try and meditate, though my head was overcrowded with disturbing memories from nearly every year of my life. Luckily, I had a lifelong training in yoga, meditation, physical therapy, and rehabilitation techniques in my bag of tricks; so in an effort to control my hysteria, I talked myself into a breathing exercise in an attempt to slow down my racing heart and brain. In just a few minutes, it was working and the mad chatter banging in my head began to slow to a discussion of sorts.

Then with my eyes still closed, I gazed upward into my third eye and began to see what I was hearing. I've always been able to visualize, but this was different—this time, someone was holding my hand and quickly reviewing my life history. I recognized places, people, and scenes as this timeline picture show presented itself. We visited the time when I was only three weeks old with a double hernia; when my brother was born at home; dancing on stage in my Hungarian dress, admiring the pretty ribbons as I twirled; then our driveway gate falling on me and crushing my eight-year-old spine, head, knees, and little body. It slowed down there for a bit as I saw myself in third grade, bandaged up and going to doctor appointments, instead of dance class. I tried so hard to pretend there was nothing wrong with me because, in my head, admitting it would make me a victim, weak and vulnerable, so I refused to admit to any pain.

With every vision that came and went, so did my breath. All of a sudden, I was drowning in the ocean after jumping into the rip tide to save my little brother; though thankfully rescued by the lifeguard, I puked up sand for days. There I was at twelve, starting college so I could graduate high school early…I was so hungry for knowledge that the jokes and criticism only fueled my determination. Then the car accidents started rolling in. I watched the time my mom ran a stop sign and a truck broadsided us; another time, we slammed into a car stopped at a green light, and on a family vacation, we were in a multi-car pile up that put me in a back brace the same month I had braces put on my teeth, lost my best friend to a drunk driver, and started public high school. I wasn't exactly approachable; in fact, I was enraged and laughed as I got kicked off the bus for knocking out a boy who tickled me after I told him to stop, once. I tolerated the system for a couple of months then went full-time at college, was chairman of the junior auxiliary at the hospital, worked odd jobs and hand made accessories and jewelry which sold at local gift shops. At that pace, I graduated high school a year later and was confident about my future. I wanted to be a doctor, specifically a neonatal surgeon.

A huge exhale of relief confirmed that I had finally gotten over that period and I started to feel a warm vibration in my spine. We moved on to how I became obsessed with exercise, strength, and speed because the more adrenaline I could rally in my body, the less pain I felt. Flash forward, and I was in a hospital bed, waking up to find out I had become anaphylactic allergic to dairy overnight and almost didn't make it. Then six months later, I was in the same hospital with walking pneumonia, frustrated that I couldn't teach my exercise classes, go to school, or work my shifts at the restaurant. Fibrocystosis developed in my breast and uterine tissues; the medications and procedures only made it worse, and I was diagnosed with acute Fibromyalgia by the time I was nineteen.

After all that demanding to the Universe, I now had my *answers*. Everything I went through was to prepare me for HELPING and TEACHING others how to heal themselves.

Whoa…the day of my first wedding. We didn't have a chance to make it, what with our family issues and his convict brother. My marriage was over and settled in less than two years, so I moved to Florida to re-identify my life and self. On a trip to Freeport, Bahamas, with my new boyfriend and a few other guys, I flat-lined from a dairy allergy poisoning in the grossest hospital I had ever seen! They jabbed the same needle into my hands and arms some 15 times trying to get a vein. I was lifted out of my body and watched as the boys threw the doctor up against the wall and threatened to end his life if he didn't save mine. Back in Palm Beach now, my boyfriend ran a red light when making a left turn, and an illegal Haitian that picked up a junkyard car just two hours earlier plowed into my side. That did it! I was wrapped in braces, on heavy narcotics, and needed a cane to walk.

Another deep whimpering inhale and exhausted exhale moved me through each memory, and I lay there numb, buzzing all over. I had never taken a tour of my life like that before, and I was in awe that the experience was over in just a few minutes. Whimpering continued, but calmer now—I still didn't understand, still didn't have my answer, and was still in that perplexing state of mind.

Pleading out loud in my silent condo (vacant to one side, deaf neighbor on the other), I felt free to express myself—granted, I had no control at this point! I pushed and pulled my body into a seated position, cushioned with pillows, and petitioned for some serious answers. "Enough already!" I yelled into the ether, "I surrender…what do you want from me?!" My trickling tears turned into white water rapids of intense desperation and panic.

It seemed like an hour had gone by, but it was probably less, when the sound of silence overwhelmed me and I looked up from the wet pillow to see this iridescent, crystalline, rainbow light bubble slowly surrounding me, then encasing me in the center of its radiant glow. Rubbing my eyes to focus clearly, it was still there, glowing with a magical presence, when I realized there was no pain. In fact, I couldn't feel my body at all! Oh my God, what relief! Looking around my bubble, the worry and sadness disappeared. Twinkling lights floated in a spiral around me, and somehow I knew I was safe and loved. So much love poured into me that my sobs of sorrow turned into tears of joy, and before I knew it, I was almost giggling! I wondered what was going on, how could my entire state of being change just like that? But I felt such joy, pure love, and intense protection that the questions stopped immediately so I could enjoy the experience—after all, I didn't know how long it would last. Taking a deep breath in, holding it for a bit, then letting it go, I fully gave in to this miraculous sphere of white rainbow light around me. I felt compelled to close my eyes and give thanks for this beautiful gift; and when I did, the same hand that guided me before took me again to see the other side of my story. This time, I saw what was happening as a result of each accident or injury—the immense learning, karma burning, and hands-on training of everything, from each physical therapy trick in the book, herbal remedies, and meditation techniques to discovering and creating dairy-free and vegetarian recipes.

Every flashback I was shown before was being replayed, but in a new light, with love and a very positive message. Instead of seeing and feeling the suffering, I saw and felt the power, strength, gratitude, and joy that I experienced as a result of each issue. The caring, love, healing, and education I received from each therapist or doctor was glowing with gratefulness. A smile began to take shape on my face, and I could feel my cheeks quivering, not sure if they were supposed to smile after being in sorrow for so long. Happiness like I had never felt before was filling the luminous bubble and infusing me with more and more joy, one beautiful scene after another. The passionate drive to heal myself from each injury and illness came from my relentless desire to dance, run, play, explore, create, learn, and prove others wrong…I can and will be healed! Many call this as the "Annatude." My smile turned to a giggle as I recognized how precious each moment was and how lucky I am to have lived through and learned from these incidences. My heart was full of joy, my body was peaceful, and my head was finally at ease.

I opened my eyes to see that the magic bubble was still all around me, loving and protecting me, and it was never going to leave. In all my 30 years, I had never been this overjoyed with happiness! It was unexplainable! The shear knowing of this gift

was beyond anything I had ever heard of, and here I was living it, soaking up every millisecond. Then another knowing came to me—it had always been here! We all have happy bubbles; we just can't see them like this all the time! I felt a warm golden light beaming from my heart and swirling with the rainbow lights of my bubble, and we were one—we've always been one.

Being born into a yogi family, I had learned how to meditate before talking and practiced my spiritual teachings and lifestyle throughout my existence. This was certainly one of the major reasons I triumphed over adversity. All I could think of now was how much I wanted to share this knowing with my friends, family, and everyone, so they, too, could see, feel, and understand this phenomenon. Taking deep peaceful breaths, I quietly drifted off and slept like a baby for the next 18 hours. When I woke, a new mission was born.

Continuing to learn how to heal myself, I knew that the 50-70 trillion cells in my body are replaced with new cells every seven years or so. My strategy and goal to be completely healed was absolutely attainable, especially with the new alliance of my happy bubble. As I researched every natural healing modality known, received treatments, and practiced the teachings I was now immersed in, my body healed at a molecular level, my brain consciousness was being reprogrammed, and my soul found harmony. In my studies, I have always searched for validation of my experience and found that many others had shared in the happy bubble vision…the great white light sphere of love is a common occurrence after all! Story after story, our unified understanding brought us together and confirmed that none of us were crazy or hallucinating, in fact, we have a divine gift to share. How amazingly special! The knowing that a greater source of energy and life exists is real, and we all have the power to access it for total healing, joy, harmony, and abundance in every way imaginable…but what is it? After years of researching the phenomenon, I finally discovered that science calls my happy bubble a toroidal field. Around the solar system, it's an electromagnetic/gravitomagnetic flux; around the earth, it's a geomagnetic field; and around our bodies, it's referred to as the human body field—they are all toroidal electromagnetic energy. The happy bubble that I exist in is now finally confirmed by science! It's been known about forever, yet not shared or taught for some reason. Of the hundred or so healers I've worked with, most knew about chakra energy, but only a few knew about toroidal energy. Electromagnetic vibrations around each chakra point align to create a center core, which generates a toroid around our bodies. Like a magnet, those who are aware of this energy feel a vibrational resonance and are immediately drawn together. As if reuniting with an old friend, we gravitate to each other and quickly pick up where we left off. It seems everyone has experienced this attraction with people in their lives.

After all that demanding to the Universe, I now had my answers. Everything I went through was to prepare me for helping and teaching others how to heal themselves using their toroidal field, natural lifestyle, holistic healing, and a compassionate attitude of gratitude. By implementation and practice of these techniques, health and happiness radiate from the individual to their family, community, and our planet as a whole. As we each learn to harness and utilize our innate energetic power, the healing exponentially increases and reaches far beyond conventional comprehension. At last, my "what, how and why's" were pleasantly revealed; my existence now has true purpose and meaning, and I give thanks for love and I am grateful for every second of my life! DM

ANNA ALLEN

Three Feet Beyond Gold

IN THE WINTER of 2009, I finished the manuscript to my first solo book project entitled *The Total Female Package,* an inspirational guidebook for women to own their value and worth in this lifetime, and my journey to conquer the world with its message began to unfold.

I had received AMAZ!NG news when my mentor, Jeff Olson, reviewed my book and shared "I would buy one for every woman I know once they are printed!" I knew at that point that I had something magical and the Universe had blessed me with the words to open people's hearts to believing in their personal power with daily practices. So I did what most would never think to do—with only six months of income in the bank to live on, I quit my job to pursue my dream of giving the world a faith-lift.

I knew I had to keep some sort of income flow, so I reached out to my network for project and part-time opportunities, while I let my internal guidance system lead me on a path to publishing my book. Then within two short weeks of my immediate departure from Corporate America, a friend emailed me about an opportunity to work with two highly successful men on a book launch. "Have you ever heard of the personal development book, Napoleon Hill's *Think & Grow Rich?*" he wrote. I wanted to reach through the email and shake him up a bit. "Of course!" That book is the all-time personal development book of how to achieve your desired results!

Well, as it turns out, the Napoleon Hill Foundation was finally allowing a second edition to be published called *Three Feet From Gold*. Co-author Greg Reid and marketing and distribution mogul Dean Kosage were teaming up to create the ultimate book launch for this classic's second coming. They were searching for a red carpet host that could hold her own to interview all of the stars of personal development. From the Secret's John Assaraf to billionaire lady LuAn Mitchell to Tony Robbins, there was an endless array of personal development celebrities being honored in this new installment, and Greg and Dean believed I would be perfect to lead and host the scene of two-minute interviews.

The event was a huge success, and as I proved myself to be a team player, I was asked to take on an additional project—one that coincidentally turned out to be my very own *Three Feet From Gold* experience. I have not only Greg Reid, but also the Napoleon Hill Foundation, to now thank for that terminology.

The project I am speaking of is the one currently in your hands. I was asked to manage and help organize this book project. Being a writer and someone in earnest desire to publish her own book, I immediately took on the new challenge with enthusiasm and inspiration. I was soon approached with the hindsight of what most entrepreneurs in the few short months after the project began, realizing that "becoming an entrepreneur is the best personal development you can ever truly do – the reason why – it brings up all of your own bullshit!"

I soon realized the lack of experience I had for creating systems and processes for duplication. I then realized that my art of being a people person and developing relationships also had a weaker side of allowing others to walk all over me at the fear of displeasing them and their expectations. I wanted everyone to be happy, fed, and honored for their beliefs, contribution, and insights, even though I had to manage so many different personalities throughout the book project.

> " I knew at that point that I had something MAGICAL and the **Universe** had blessed me with the words to open people's hearts to believing in their ***personal power*** with daily practices. "

In the beginning, the project was rolling! We had very excited people who were extremely eager to be a part of a new coffee table book by sharing their defining moment and becoming published as an author. We held several conference calls and gatherings to showcase Greg Reid and Dean Kosage as the masterminds behind the scenes of this soon-to-be-amazing new series! People expressed genuine interest, and within the first month, I had found two of our first authors within my personal network. I was over the moon!

And then what happened next is what tends to happen to most of us…I let life get in the way of completing the project. Almost two years after its start, it was finally being birthed so it could be received by your hands and your eyes now.

You may be wondering what happened during those two years. What got in the way of you completing the project? Well, there were many learning moments, but I took something away from each—the conviction to never give up! In the back of my mind, I was always thinking about the book project and eager to have it completed with the best-of-the-best stories. I believed in the vision Dean Kosage had once shared with me many months prior and kept striving toward it....even after the following moments came to fruition:

- I had been hand selected to help create a brand new coaching and personal development training company called Freestyle.
- I had decided to dissolve a separate business partnership and had to walk through the entire legal process, which took many months.
- The economic recession took a hit on my real estate investments, and I had to make some new decisions on how to move forward.
- I had to recruit and find an additional project manager to help me complete this book project since my attention was being pulled in other directions. I went through three project managers until I stumbled upon Cynthia Luois, who has now been the backbone to help me become organized, interview authors for the book, update our website, and be the liaison to our wonderful and patient editor, Patti McKenna.
- Greg Reid decided to leave the book project to begin his own publishing company with his wife, Allyn.
- Dean Kosage and I were asked to speak on a tour in Australia and around North

America at various corporations about global trends.

- The quickening of constant technology upgrades was beginning to affect thousands of people we train, so we had to plan how to educate and make those not as comfortable feel safe. For those who were comfortable, we had to make sure they were utilizing the tools to develop their business and self-worth appropriately.
- I published my book, *The Total Female Package.*
- My story was published in Jeff Olson's new edition of *The Slight Edge.*
- And so on and so on...

You see, what folks forget to realize in life is that it is happening all the time and in every form. When you take on a project and make a commitment to be in service to your trusting clients, your integrity is on the line.

The things I learned in this book project continue to be an example in my life.

My defining moment came from never giving up – seeing it through and literally taking the masterpiece of one of Napoleon Hill's all-time greatest works and making it my modern day journey.

What you have in your hands is a product of deep love, respect, and the attitude to keep pursuing your dreams even when others around you want you to give up. You are the only person who can hold yourself accountable and allow yourself to experience *Three Feet BEYOND Gold*. Get after it! DM

NOVALENA J. BETANCOURT

BREAKING FREE FROM

Other People's Dogma

THE LIFE OF A PIRATE

WHEN I WAS LITTLE, my younger brother, Dan, and I lived a life on the ocean with my mother and her boyfriend. My childhood, much different than most, was fostered in a life as a modern day pirate. We ran a sailboat off the coast of Florida and always had many interesting travelers on board, from the extremely wealthy to action-seeking Miami Vice characters. With so many stories boarding our sailboats, I was always in deep observation of human patterns and behaviors.

I grew up with no sense of time beyond sunrise and sunset, literally not knowing what day of the week it was. My time measurements, versus calendars, were events and memories. As you can imagine, my current paradigm has been shaped and molded from a very different upbringing than most. To this day, I believe growing up without most of society's dogma allowed me to think and dream outside of the box.

PATTERN RECOGNITION

Two major things impacted my attention to recognizing human behavioral patterns at an early age:

1. Growing up on the ocean demands an instant respect for nature. It doesn't matter if you are 6 or 16, the ocean will expect you to pay very close attention to her. Many kids today are very sheltered from the basic survival skills that create a sustainable human being. This often leads to a lack of self-worth and dependency on others.

2. I was raised by smugglers. Some of my youngest memories include being coached on how to evade the police and decode phone messages. At six and seven years old, this was a lot of responsibility for my brother and me. It's also very confusing when you can't tell people what your parents do for a living at a time when you're trying to figure out what life is about.

Although these skills were unusual for my age, they set me decades ahead of my friends in high school. I had already lived as a pirate, became self-sustainable, and had lived in a foreign country. Those early experiences had exposed me to other worlds and belief systems.

When I was thrown into our educational system for the first time, I was in quite a shock after living off the matrix for so long. I instantly noticed I was being taught memorization techniques versus life skills by some people who had no self-sustainable skills of their own. And while I enjoyed the social life in high school, it was clear that outdated information and styles were being taught to us, as well as beliefs outside my own. I knew in my heart there had to be another way. On sailboats, I'd seen and heard too many stories about creating and experiencing success. Four years of taking multiple-choice tests did not seem the way for me to reach my success quotient.

I started searching for mentors and sustainability in my life. I'd always dreamed of finding a successful coach who could help me discover my potential. Like so many people, I wanted to make my mark on the world and make a difference. Years of living on the water and not being able to tell anyone what my mother did had sparked my desire to do something for which I could be proud.

" I chose to follow my own **convictions** and **faith** and not be a *victim* to another's DOGMA. "

I eventually found a mentor, Mark Boyson, in a coaching and educational training company called the World Wide Group. WOW! He introduced me to more successful individuals than I could count. Although everything in the group didn't resonate with me, it was the best place I had seen at that point on my journey to learn some life skills. At the age of 20, I had a chance to become someone. I could shape my own life with my own vision and help others do the same.

THE RISE TO SUCCESS

Many people attempt things and many fail, but I grew my self-image and confidence by helping others achieve their goals each week. As I surpassed hundreds of thousands of people with better educations and social status than me, I realized I was worthy,

"Your time is limited, so don't waste it living someone else's life. Don't be trapped by dogma - which is living with the results of other people's thinking.

Don't let the noise of others' opinions drown out your own inner voice. And most important, have the courage to follow your heart and intuition.

STEVE JOBS

despite my unusual background. After a few years of hard work, I was in the .0002% of the largest and most successful network marketing company in the world.

By the age of 23, I was recognized across global stages and making a sustainable monthly income most people never experience. I had built one of the largest social networks across multiple countries, and I am very thankful to the World Wide Group for this early education.

The more folks I engaged with, the more mistakes and the more success I experienced. Extensive traveling and dealing with people with many diverse backgrounds helped me see trends most people were unable to comprehend. I became known as a prophet to some, a foreteller to others. I don't believe this is unique to me—I believe anyone who is blessed with similar experiences of travel will also discover wonderful insights and fits of clarity to share.

THE CULTURE CLASH

The information I began to discover and share with my teams at the World Wide Group when I returned from speaking across global stages was current and relevant. It revealed how people could approach their business and add value to their life with worldly insight.

As excitement grew, my newfound influence concerned my mentors. In any business, leadership that does not keep up with the pulse of the world or their own people's desires becomes disconnected from their own teams. Current credibility shifts from existing leaders to the emerging talent, which scares some because they can no longer relate.

The organization in which I had found mentors and created tremendous success had been established before the free flow of information that social media and the Internet has brought to us. Although these were wonderful people, the generation gap was making it difficult to keep up with the speed of technological improvements that allow people to collaborate and communicate across oceans. I can only imagine how difficult it must be to build a business you love for over three decades and see how the generational differences begin to play a role in its attrition if you are not ready to change.

To make things even more difficult, many leaders had woven their personal religious beliefs into their organizations to the point that it was unfortunately alienating people of other faiths. As the world was becoming more connected, this was proving to be a challenge.

DOGMA THINKING VS. CULTURE

I soon realized the culture I grew up in of shared values, attitudes and goals was no longer allowing my teams and me to grow. When I voiced my own choices and beliefs about how to lead and influence people, I learned that this was not in alignment with that culture. At that moment, I realized the organization I grew up in fostered dependency rather than encouraging business owners to truly be independent.

In the matter of what seemed like a heartbeat, I was at a major turning point in my life. The same organization that helped me achieve my success was not ready to embrace new ways to grow our businesses and expand sustainability using technology. It suddenly felt like many members of the organization where playing not to lose vs. playing to win. The same mentors who gave me books about changing my stars, being flexible, and never giving up were not living up to those same practices. Protecting what they had built was more important in their stage of life than remembering how

they built their kingdoms.

THE QUICKENING

The reluctance to embrace technology, as well as an inability to relate to the younger generation, caused me to be perceived as a threat and a distraction. Fear of change and the unknown gave birth to slander, passing judgment, and gossip. However, one individual didn't fall prey to criticism and threats—Mark Boyson, my original mentor.

OUTGROWING YOUR MENTORS

My foresight on the climate of the world and developing specific learning tools for various modalities was being recognized within many industries outside of my own. Suddenly many of the famous speakers and authors I had learned from were asking me to help them adjust to changes and trends in the world. My passion for growing businesses through the continuing changes in technology and reaching a new generation where they live had lent itself to a new expertise while many in my industry remained stuck in their way of doing business. After maturing and becoming a father, I didn't want to create dependency in people. I truly wanted to give them wings, even if they left my business to pursue other passions. Hopefully, I could be part of their lives and give them the confidence to pursue their next big passions!

THE MOMENT OF COURAGE

I could walk away from the World Wide Group, even if it meant sacrificing a substantial portion of my income and thousands of relationships. Or I could stay, keep my income, and live by a belief system for which I could not be a messenger. This transition should have been a celebration or a graduation. However, as Ken Blanchard told me personally, "Unfortunately, most organizations do not have in place any graceful way to get off the bus."

After meeting with 20 of the top authors, pastors, and leaders, it was clear to me that I needed to follow my own convictions and faith and not be a victim to another's dogma. As one pastor said when I was seeking advice on this decision,

"Dean, when you were 20 years old, you had the courage to enter a business most people did not understand, you beat the odds and made something of yourself. The only reason you would stay in this organization that no longer fits your culture is because of fear or because of allowing money to control you. I hope you have more courage and integrity now than you did at the age of 20. "

THE ROAD LESS TRAVELED

I took the road less traveled. I took a step back in lifestyle and income, restructured my business to fit my new beliefs, and discovered a new Dean—one who was much happier with himself and compassionate to others.

If you've ever made a decision that you knew was right, but you knew was going to be meet with massive resistance, I honor you. If you have ever had to break away from religion to find your own voice or personal faith, I can sympathize. Friends and colleagues can suddenly and surprisingly fade away—yet people more aligned with your new path suddenly show up, and, wow, are they a breath of fresh air!

THE LESSON

I have an ability to foresee what is coming. I know that the answer for me is to always listen to my heart, my inner voice, and even if it means experiencing ridicule from folks who oppose my forecast, doing what feels right and in service to others is the best contribution I can offer today.

Additionally, through discovering the art of listening to my inner voice, I realized I needed to let go of some relationships that were no longer serving me to allow room for the people I needed to show up in my life. There is a world of emerging talent, like the authors featured in this book or potentially you, the reader, who is looking for inspiration to take your next step of courage forward. So if you want to awaken the Giant within, let the world know. "Behold, here comes a Dreamer, and if you stand too close to me, you will catch my dream!" DM

DEAN KOSAGE

" Behold, here comes a **Dreamer**,

and if you stand too close to me, you will

catch my DREAM! "

Afterword

This book holds a collection of people who found **COURAGE** during a defining moment in their life. We hope as you read the stories in this book, you found one or two that resonated with your current step now and gave you a faith lift to make a **decision** today that Sharon would say,

"...may direct the rest of your life."

We would love to learn more about the **Defining Moments** in your life. Your story could be the turning point for another individual that encourages the hope he or she needs to ***continue*** on their path to success.

Please visit us at
www.definingmomentsbooks.com
if you would like to have your story published in our next book series.

Love,
Dean Kosage & Novalena J. Betancourt

Biographies

ALI *zaidi*: As the youngest of three children, Ali Zaidi was the only son born to his parents. His family lived in Queens, New York in the early 80's, before moving to New Jersey, where he spent most of his life. Ali Zaidi attended Rutgers University, where he received his Bachelor's in Science in Public Health/Medicine and Economics. Currently he resides in Houston, Texas, where he has received numerous awards as a sales and marketing executive with various corporations. Today, Ali Zaidi applies his talent to his own real estate firm in Houston, where he is making his mark in the industry.

ANNA *"naturalista" allen*: Founder of Natural Living Source, is an expert educator, speaker and consultant in holistic healing, environmental consciousness, Yoga lifestyle, compassionate culture, and overall sustainability for the individual, family, community, workplace and our planet. Anna is Program Director at The Center For Living In Harmony, "a nonprofit organization dedicated to the promotion of Self-Reliant, Harmonious Living," and Vice President of Lean & Green Kids, "empowering our youth to make a difference in their own lives, and in their world…" through awareness of healthy food choices. Anna's miraculous healings empowered her to share her awareness with the world. www.NaturalLivingSource.com

BRAD *dehaven***:** Resides in San Diego, California with his family. Brad speaks at conferences around the world as an advocate and teacher of success principles for entrepreneurs. He has inspired over 1 million people on 5 continents through live events and his bestselling book, *The Currency of the Future*, has sold over 250,000 copies. Brad mentors and coaches new young entrepreneurs and start-ups. He is also the founder of MotiVision Media: "Tools for Life" and the co-founder of his newest project, "MyFootballMentor.com," a website geared for the development of young athletes.

CYNTHIA *luois***:** Activist, feminist, public speaker and entrepreneur, Cynthia Luois earned two bachelor's degrees at the University of Arizona in 2010. She also co-founded and is the current Managing Partner of Assessment and Plan Lifestyle Design (APLD) Consultation Services, based in Los Angeles, California. Her work is centered on helping people – especially women – empower and elevate all circles of their lives. Cynthia is deeply committed to enhancing quality of life and stopping violence against women across the globe. Originally from Arizona, Cynthia currently resides in Los Angeles with her partner, Mahdi Pessarakli. Contact Cynthia for consultation services, via email: Cyn@APLDConsult.com.

CRYSTAL *berg***:** Crystal is a graduate of Chapman University and has been involved in orphan care and education initiatives around the world. She is the co-founder of True Life, an organization focused on life-changing experiences for people throughout the U.S. and Canada. Originally from the Northwest, Crystal and her husband have made Southern California their home. Passionate about seeing every person reach their God-given potential, they spend their time developing spiritual growth and international volunteer opportunities, in addition to writing books and curriculum for group studies. Author Website: http://www.crystal-berg.com

DEAN *kosage*: Dean Kosage is the founder of Freestyle, Inc. Many leaders in many industries have recognized him as a person of notable influence. Dean is the founder of Zooplr, a gamification learning management system, and is also the mastermind behind Defining Moments Publishing, a company that helps emerging talent become published authors. You can learn more about Dean at www.deankosage.com.

DENICE *morales kennedy*: The entrepreneurial bug bit Denice in her mid-twenties. After 10 years in sales and marketing, she listened to her little voice and stepped out on her own. Finding her niche in consulting individuals and businesses in revenue enhancement, that is where she fell in love with the networking industry. Being her own boss and living life on her terms, Denice started a boutique consulting firm and a networking business that has created a family legacy. Her business encompasses opportunity, family, friends, travel, hope and reward. For over 30 years, she has been helping people live life on their own terms. Contact Denice at dmkennedy6@gmail.com.

DOMINIC *mckenna*: Dominic McKenna is a business owner, speaker, and coach from Melbourne, Australia. He is a second-generation entrepreneur and ambassador in his family's network marketing business. He speaks around Australia on marketing, branding, and empowerment. Dom's greatest passions are the sport of CrossFit and Team Mak Youth Camp, a youth program he has been running annually for the last 5 years. The camp has enabled him to connect with over 600 Australian youth and help them achieve their goals and realize their dreams. For more information on Dom, visit his personal blog at www.DomMcKenna.com.

GARY *adamson***:** Gary Adamson, Chief Experience Officer of Starizon Studio, began his career in 1978 as Vice-President of Swedish Health Systems in Denver, where he started the nation's first and most comprehensive hospital-based wellness program. In 1999, he co-founded Starizon Studio to help organizations design transforming experiences and strengthen their brand success. A highly rated speaker at regional, national, and international conferences, Gary is also co-author of The Complete* Guide to Transforming the Patient Experience (HCPro, 2009). He received his Masters Degree in Health Administration from the University of Colorado, and his undergraduate degree is from the University of Notre Dame.

HEATHER *blaise***:** Since retiring as Vice President of Operations for Quizno's Subs and Director of Operations of Taco Bell, Heather Blaise speaks at universities about running successful businesses. Feeling it is her duty to inspire others, she shares that everything is possible. A creative soul, Heather has studied fashion since childhood and is a fashion stylist, gardener, artist, and writer. Born in N.Y. and raised all over Canada, Heather is now living in San Diego. She is fluent in French, English, speaks a little Spanish, and is currently learning Brazilian Portuguese. Heather has four blogs, including www.yourinstyleguru.com, and www.heatherblaise.com.

HUSEIN *malik***:** Husein Malik is an emerging coach on leadership, business, and personal development, having publicly spoken to thousands of listeners in multiple languages on subjects ranging from business to spirituality. He now dedicates his life to teaching and inspiring others to live a life of purpose while continuing to open the doors for many into the world of personal development and self-sustainability. He is studying to be a business coach at the Social Business School and is helping to develop a 21st century, cutting-edge system to help others around the globe achieve greatness and live their ultimate life.

JEREMY *nichele*: Equipped with a solid background in business and marketing, Jeremy Nichele has become a successful entrepreneur and team leader. Before co-founding and becoming CEO of Wonton Media Inc., Jeremy served as CEO of both The Bucket List Project and Macro Media Marketing, Inc. He also received the exclusive "Rookie of the Year" award at Excel Telecom, where he served as an Executive Director. Jeremy has learned that inspiration blossoms from thinking big, realizing your dreams require passion and dedication, and that success is a product of hard play and team work. You can contact Jeremy at Jeremy@Wonton.com.

JOSEPH *moffett*: A former Marine, personal trainer, and entrepreneur, Joe Moffett is now on the path to building an empire in the personal growth/mentorship world. After 5 years in the Marine Corps, traveling to various countries all over the world, and a tour in Iraq serving our country, at age 26, Joe is helping others unleash the power within them and magnify their dreams. He is helping others strip the layers of life to get to the core of their defining moment. You can contact Joe at JoeMoffettWCM@gmail.com.

JOHNATHAN *l. perryman*: Johnathan L. Perryman is an entrepreneur and a businessman. The second of three children, he was born on April 25, 1974, in Carmel,

California to Paula Torrente and Eddie Perryman. Johnathan attended the University of Nevada-Reno and graduated from the University of Mary (Bismarck, ND) with a Masters Degree in Physical Therapy in 2000. In addition to being a physical therapist, he has been an entrepreneur and businessman since 2003. Johnathan married Noel Nichols on June 28, 1997, and the couple lives in Reno, Nevada with their two children.

KARLA *j. pinckes:* Karla J. Pinckes is an attorney and the Business Contracts Manager for The Ken Blanchard Companies. She oversees contract negotiations with Blanchard's domestic and international direct and indirect sales relationships. She graduated with honors from The University of San Diego with a Master's of Science in Executive Leadership and is a member of Beta Gamma Sigma, an international honor society. Karla is also Co-Chair of the International Law Section of the San Diego County Bar Association and sits on the Board of Directors of the New Children's Museum. She lives in Encinitas with her husband, Michael, and her two children, Caden and Addison.

LILLIAN *razavi:* Lillian Razavi began her professional career in banking and insurance at the age of 16. She has also served on various boards and committees in her communities. Lillian founded and served as president elect of the Rotary Club of Mission Valley Sunset and is a board member of the Rotary Club of Antioch. In 2005, she founded Future Women CEOs to empower collegiate women. Lillian received the Entrepreneurial Value award from the Lloyd Grief Center for Entrepreneurship at the University of Southern California. A native Californian, she graduated from USC with a degree in business administration, finance and entrepreneurship.

DR. MOHAMMAD *mahdi pessarakli:* Dr. Mohammad Mahdi Pessarakli is a quality of life activist, physician, and serial entrepreneur from Tucson, Arizona. He completed his undergraduate and medical education in his hometown, attending The University of Arizona. He is a Principal of Assessment and Plan Lifestyle Design (APLD) Consultation Services, based in Los Angeles, California. He will become Chief Medical Officer for APLD in mid-2012. Meanwhile, he is undergoing specialty training in The University of Southern California's Pathology (AP/CP) program. Dr. Pessarakli currently resides in Downtown Los Angeles with his partner, Cynthia Luois. Contact Dr. Pessarakli via the email address available at www.pessarakli.com.

MIKE *somerville***:** Mike Somerville is the CEO and founder of AMAZING, LLC a world-class life transformation company. He earned his Bachelor of Science in Electrical Engineering from San Diego State University and Master of Science in Executive Leadership from The University of San Diego. Mike has owned several IT consulting companies in San Diego and San Felipe, Mexico. Prior to that time, he worked in the radio and entertainment industry. Mike is on the board of several organizations and is a guest speaker for bachelor and masters classes on entrepreneurship and leadership. Visit his website at www.AmazingLife.us .

NOVALENA *j. betancourt:* A global change agent, author, speaker, experiential coach, and leadership trainer for business owners developing high-performing teams. Novalena wrote *The Total Female Package*, an inspirational guidebook and audio series to help women live in authentic ownership of their value and self-worth. She co-authored *Strategies for Success* with Jack Canfield and Marie Diamond of *The Secret.* Novalena became a partner of Defining Moments Publishing and is a leader at Freestyle, Inc., helping folks fund their dreams through social business. Her background includes a Master's of Science in Executive Leadership at the University of San Diego. www. thetotalfemalepackage.com

ROCHELLE *patterson:* As a wife, mother, and entrepreneur, Rochelle Patterson is gaining financial freedom and the freedom to live life her way through self-growth and education in specialized skills. After partnering with The West Coast Movement and Freestyle, she is doing what it takes to be a better leader and example to her family and her team. Today, Rochelle helps other women learn how to embrace their talents and abilities and become better business owners in order to live out their dreams and aspirations. You can contact Rochelle at rmpattersonwcm@gmail.com.

RODNEY *kesling:* Living in Manhattan Beach, CA with his wife Danielle, a former LPGA Touring Professional, and their two children, Rod is a renowned information security consultant and entrepreneur. His client list includes the U.S. Government and the top satellite companies in the country, including Lockheed Martin, Northrup Grumman, Boeing, Loral, and others. In 2011, Rod and Danielle formed Kesling Trilogy Solutions to enable entrepreneurial minded people the ability to fund their passions and create life by design. Information on Kesling Trilogy Solutions can be found at www.facebook.com/keslingtrilogysolutions, and Rod may be reached at rod@keslingtrilogy.com

SARAH *koops vanderveen:* A writer and blogger living in Laguna Beach, California. She is the former editor of The Mars Hill Review, a literary journal focused on the intersection of faith and culture, and Krakoosh magazine, a content-driven catalog emphasizing adventure sports. She is currently at work on two books, a volume of poetry inspired by her poetry blog, Once By the Pacific, and a memoir. She lives with her husband, David, and their two teenage sons, Schuyler and Willem. When she's not writing, she does lots of laundry, surfs, and plays tennis with her family.

SHARON *lechter:* As an entrepreneur, author, philanthropist, educator, international speaker, licensed CPA and mother. Co-author of *Think and Grow Rich-Three Feet From Gold, Rich Dad Poor Dad* and 14 other books, Sharon annotated and updated *Outwitting the Devil* by Napoleon Hill. She founded Pay Your Family First to empower prosperous futures through financial literacy education. Sharon is national spokesperson for the National CPAs Commission on Financial Literacy, instructor for Thunderbird School of Global Management's Project Artemis, and served on the first President's Advisory Council on Financial Literacy, and boards of Childhelp, Women Presidents' Organization, and EmpowHer. Visit www.sharonlechter.com.

PATTI *mckenna*: A ghostwriter, author, and editor, Patti McKenna has worked in the self-help, professional and personal development industries for ten years. She is the author of *Caution: Children Should Come With Warning Labels* and *From a Lullaby to Goodbye, Comfort and Support for Grieving Parents.* McKenna has edited countless books and ghosted bestselling business and non-fiction books, as well as memoirs. She can be reached via email: PcMcKenna6@aol.com.